EVALUATING LIBRARY INSTRUCTION

SAMPLE QUESTIONS, FORMS, AND STRATEGIES FOR PRACTICAL USE

RESEARCH COMMITTEE, LIBRARY INSTRUCTION ROUND TABLE
AMERICAN LIBRARY ASSOCIATION

EDITED BY DIANA D. SHONROCK

American Library Association
Chicago and London
1996

f the library's General Reference Section at
niversity in Ames, Diana Shonrock has more
ears' experience in library instruction. In addi-
adership in LIRT, she is active in the Bibliographic Instruction Section of ALA's Association of College
and Research Libraries.

Project editor: Louise Howe

Cover design: Ellen Scanlon

Text design: Dianne M. Rooney

Composition by Publishing Services, Inc.
in Times and Antique Olive
using Xyvision/Linotype L330

Printed on 50-pound Publisher Smooth, a pH-neutral
stock, and bound in 10-point C1S cover stock by
McNaughton & Gunn, Inc.

The paper used in this publication meets the minimum
requirements of American National Standard for
Information Sciences—Permanence of Paper for
Printed Library Materials, ANSI Z39.48-1992.∞

Library of Congress Cataloging-in-Publication Data

Evaluating library instruction : sample questions,
    forms, and strategies for practical use / Research
    Committee, Library Instruction Round Table,
    American Library Association ; edited by Diana D.
    Shonrock.
        p.   cm.
    Includes bibliographical references and index.
    ISBN 0-8389-0665-6 (alk. paper)
    1. Library orientation—United States—
Evaluation.   I. Shonrock, Diana D.   II. American
Library Association. Library Instruction Round
Table. Research Committee.
Z711.2.E894   1996
025.5′6—dc20   95-23608

Contents

Preface

ne major role of the American Library Association Library Instruction Round Table (LIRT) is contributing to the excellence of library instruction in all types of libraries. The LIRT Research Committee is charged with identifying, reviewing, and disseminating information about substantive, state-of-the-art research in the field of library instruction and with pinpointing areas where research needs to be developed. All areas of library and information science benefit from introspective analysis and research, and the LIRT Research Committee has a rich history in both areas.

Traditionally, LIRT has emphasized means by which individual instruction librarians may assess their programs and services. Assessment can be done through consultation, case study, and survey research. Clearly, survey research has enjoyed the broadest popularity among librarians, as it is a convenient way to collect information. To assist library instruction librarians in gathering information about their programs from users, we have created a handbook of model questions that can be used to develop surveys and evaluation instruments tailored to individual settings.

History of the Handbook

Over the years the LIRT Research Committee has undertaken numerous projects to assist librarians in evaluating what they do more effectively. During the summer 1991 ALA meetings, the committee began to discuss a new project. Having recently completed a research project/survey to determine how and why librarians do instruction,[1] the committee decided that it next wanted to encourage useful and ongoing research relating to library instruction through an instrument that was already widely used, the evaluation form. Specifically, members hoped to promote the view that library instruction evaluation is undertaken not merely to support librarians' performance appraisal, but as research that is integral to the instruction process. The committee began a literature review of articles about library instruction evaluation and issued a request for sample evaluation forms from the readers of the *LIRT Newsletter, C&RL News,* and the *LOEX News.* About seventy-five sample evaluation forms were soon received.

As indicated by the minutes from the 1991 meeting in Atlanta, the committee originally intended to develop model library instruction evaluation forms along with accompanying research on why certain questions and formats provide more reliable research results than others. Its goals and objectives indicated that the sample forms would serve both as a research tool to critique evaluation forms and as a basis for a series of articles discussing how evaluation of library programs can produce research articles.

The committee began by dividing the sample evaluation forms into three categories: evaluation of instructors, evaluation of class work, and evaluation of materials and equipment as related to library instruction. Next these three groups of questionnaires were subdivided by the types of libraries represented by the LIRT membership: public, special, school, and academic.

Sample questionnaires were then critiqued to select qualities and questions worthy of inclusion in a model survey or evaluation form, and the literature review continued. During this time, the number of sample survey/evaluation forms received increased to nearly 300, and the question arose of the best way to focus the project: should the committee concentrate on a single type of evaluation, such as student evaluation of the instructor or of handouts, or should it develop various types of surveys simultaneously?

---

1. Emily Bergman and Lill Maman, "Aims of User Education: Special Library Results," *Special Libraries* 83 (Summer 1992): 156–62.

As the number of sample questions grew, the committee began to examine the feasibility of creating a handbook of sample evaluation questions for all types of libraries and library environments. First the committee categorized the questions and put them in an electronic format. Individual members entered portions of the questions on disks and initiated the process of eliminating duplication. Next, Julie Todaro entered all the items into a single data file in a number of subsections defined by the area of instruction covered, and the committee commenced the enormous task of trying to determine which questions were applicable to which types of libraries.

During the 1993 summer ALA meeting, the focus of the committee's discussion turned to developing a database of questions that could be assembled in multiple ways and used in multiple types of libraries and library-related situations. The development of this database necessitated not only further sectioning and weeding of existing questions but also adding new questions to address the electronic formats that were being introduced in libraries. Aware of the need for help in designing evaluation forms and heeding the maxim "never reinvent the wheel," the LIRT Research Committee set its charge as follows:

- discuss and analyze the need in the field;
- design a plan of action;
- gather documents already in use;
- analyze the instruments gathered;
- revise the plan based on the determined need;
- provide information as required;
- compile the questions in usable formats;
- compile model questionnaires; and
- publish and disseminate the information.

This plan seemed ambitious in terms of the amount of information to be gathered, the analysis necessary to make it useful, and the creation of the final product, but the committee felt it was a worthwhile project with achievable results. The handbook that eventually resulted from this plan includes:

A simple guide to developing, conducting, and tabulating a survey or evaluation of library services and programs relating to instruction.

Fourteen sections of sample questions that can be used in various settings.

Four appendixes, containing:

    A. a sample cover letter;

    B. sample attitudinal and measurement scales;

    C. pre- and post-instruction checklists; and

    D. a number of sample evaluation forms developed from this handbook.

A glossary of terms relating to evaluation.

A bibliography of easy-to-read books, chapters, and articles that discuss various aspects of evaluation.

A mail-in evaluation form for the handbook itself.

The final form of this handbook is largely the work of the editor and current chair of the committee, Diana Shonrock. She wrote the introductory matter and many of the section introductions, edited the contributions of other committee members and coordinated their responses to the text, and compiled most of the material in the appendixes.

Acknowledgments

his handbook is the collective effort of hundreds of library instruction librarians. The editor and the LIRT Research Committee are grateful for the advice and counsel of all of them. Special thanks go to:

Everyone who shared sample evaluation forms with the committee.

Members of the LIRT Research Committee past and present.

Previous Research Committee chairs during this project: Emily Bergman, Cindy Schatz, and Rebecca Gardner.

The LIRT Executive Board.

Those special people who gave of their time to read, reread, and pretest this handbook.

The Public Services Division of the Iowa State University Library, which provided me with research time for completing this project.

Particularly, my husband, Bill, and my family, for enduring.

All of us on the committee sincerely hope that you will find this handbook helpful in suppressing the urge to postpone evaluation of your programs and services until you have more time; that time won't come. We hope, too, that you will be encouraged to begin ongoing library instruction research as an outgrowth of this evaluation process.

Current LIRT Research Committee members:

Mary C. Clarkson
  Trinity University

Sherry DeDecker
  University of California, Santa Barbara

Jim Kapoun
  Southwest State University

Kari Lucas
  University of California, San Diego

Lorna Peterson
  SUNY, Buffalo

Margaret Phillips
  University of California, Berkeley

Sharon L. Stewart
  University of Alabama, Tuscaloosa

Julie Todaro
  Austin Community College, Texas

Diana D. Shonrock
Iowa State University, Ames
Chair, LIRT Research Committee

Introduction

There are three basic steps involved in library instruction: first, determine the needs; second, design the program; and third, evaluate the result to see if it met the predetermined needs. This practical handbook focuses mainly on the third step, but because evaluation must be considered when planning, it also assists in the design of library instruction. Devising the evaluation *before* the instruction takes place will help you to prepare a clear, coherent presentation.

The hundreds of questions in the fourteen sections of this handbook can be used to design a variety of instruments ranging from pretests, to evaluation of a workshop, formative evaluation of a videotape, or summative evaluation of a semester course. The questions were gathered from instruments used by librarians around the country and then revised, expanded, and updated to provide models applicable to a variety of situations in all types of libraries. The handbook also provides many useful aids to developing an evaluation process, among them:

- some simple suggestions on tabulating the information gathered;
- an appendix containing acceptable, tested response points for attitude and measurement scales;
- a selective glossary of terms from the literature as used in this handbook;
- an appendix containing sample evaluation forms devised using questions from this handbook; and
- a bibliography of practical materials related to writing goals and objectives and developing evaluations.

Planning to Evaluate Library Instruction

The Purpose of Evaluation

The hard data that librarians need to support decisions are often difficult to collect in service environments where users may not interact directly with the staff even when they benefit from the information or resources. Yet such data are crucial for accountability and decision making in library instruction. It answers questions such as: "How well did we do this?" "How can we better allocate our resources?" "Where can we make changes or improve?" Surveys and evaluations are proven ways to gather data. A well-written, successfully executed survey or evaluation contributes to an organization's self-analysis by providing useful, realistic information that reflects activity and use, as well as data on facilities, publicity, programs, expertise, and services.

Proper Planning

Planning is probably the most important and most neglected part of any library services program. Creating effective and useful assessment instruments requires both intent and forethought.

> *Intent*—knowing what you want to accomplish before you set out a plan.
>
> *Forethought*—planning through mental formulation.

Proper prior planning avoids pitfalls! Develop a strategy that will ensure the best possible results from your evaluation instrument. Ask yourself:

What do I want to know?

How can I gather this information?

How will I use this information?

The first of these questions is addressed through "needs assessment."

Needs Assessment

Anne Roberts states that the results of needs assessment should tell you:

who the users are,

what they already know,

what they don't know, and

what they want to be able to do.[1]

Needs assessment can take many forms. Here it will be used to define the goals and objectives of the program by determining the participants' level of knowledge prior to the library instruction program or project. For student patrons this can be accomplished by consulting a teacher familiar with the problems they are having in their writing or what skills they need to write a paper appropriate to their educational level. Other examples of needs assessment include a short pretest of students' library skills to determine their research ability or a survey of public library users to learn their perceptions of their programming needs. Once the needs are understood you can establish instructional goals and objectives and devise an instrument to measure your progress. Note that evaluation must be part of the planning process if presentations, workshops, or classes are to be effective.

Goals and Objectives

Writing goals and objectives for a survey or evaluation forces the librarian, teacher, or presenter to organize material into successive increments. According to Roberts, goals are the highest ends one strives to attain. Yet goals must be stated in terms of specific and realistic results. Objectives are the activities outlined in the action plan; they define the specific results mentioned in the goals. An objective states the specific criteria of acceptable performance so that goals can be recognized and achieved, and performance and growth can be measured.

Evaluation tells us what has happened after we acted, and whether or not we achieved what we set out to do. When evaluation is built into goals and objectives from the beginning, it allows us to assess their realization. Virginia Tiefel observes that an objective has three characteristics:

performance—what the learner is able to do, the task;

conditions—conditions under which the performance is expected to occur;

criterion—quality or level of performance that is acceptable.[2]

These characteristics of objectives are delineated in the boxed example below.

Goal:	All freshmen students can use the \<Blank\> Library to locate material for a research project.
Objective:	Following a demonstration of the online catalog, students will be able to:
Performance:	conduct searches in the online catalog
	list the steps to be followed in using the online catalog
	describe the limitations of the catalog
	identify the parts of a bibliographic record.
Conditions:	Following a 1-hour demonstration of the online catalog
Criterion:	successfully complete an author search, a title search, a subject search, and a keyword search within 30 minutes.

1. Anne F. Roberts, "Writing General and Performance Objectives for Curriculum Development," in *Teaching Librarians to Teach: On-the-Job Training for Bibliographic Instruction Librarians,* edited by Alice S. Clark and Kay F. Jones (Metuchen, N.J.: Scarecrow Press, 1986), p. 47.

2. Virginia Tiefel, "Evaluating in Terms of Established Goals and Objectives," in *Evaluating Bibliographic Instruction: A Handbook* (Chicago: American Library Association, 1983), pp. 28–29.

When writing objectives, use verbs that detail action, such as "write," "select," "list," or "name." When objectives are written in terms that are easy to verify, evaluation becomes a natural part of the planning process.

Resources are also involved in achieving objectives.[3] These include time, money, people, and materials.

The Evaluation Process: Ten Basic Steps

Evaluation of library instruction materials, programs, and sessions can occur at various times before, during, and after their development and presentation. The two basic forms of evaluation are formative and summative. Formative evaluation collects data about materials and programs as they are being developed. Often applied to print handouts, audio- or videotapes, and computer-aided instruction, it allows developers to modify such products and make them more effective. Summative evaluation is conducted after a presentation or product has been introduced, to determine its success; it is often used with instruction programs, workshops, or supporting materials.[4] Regardless of when the evaluation is conducted, it should be *devised* before the instruction or program takes place.

Items in any questionnaire, survey, or evaluation must be both reliable and valid. "Reliability" refers to the degree to which the same instrument will produce the same results on different occasions, and requires that each question have the same meaning to all respondents. "Validity" assumes that the respondent is qualified to answer the questions and that all questions cover the content of the session to be evaluated.[5] Although items in this handbook have not been tested individually, they have been examined for style and format that yield both reliability and validity when used in appropriate situations.

Busy librarians may find the idea of undertaking surveys or evaluation research projects to be daunting. They should bear in mind that such activities:

- need not be massive or all-inclusive, but should be targeted and focused.

- need not be created from scratch, but instead can use questions as well as design and analysis techniques from other successful survey instruments.

- can be conducted through observation, interview, direct mail, follow-up to instruction, and many other ways.

- can be implemented at various times: following programs or instruction, before designing or pretesting a program, or at intervals during a course.

There are ten basic steps in designing program surveys or evaluations:

1. *Determine why you need to do a survey or evaluation.*

   To justify new signs or a new position? To plan for redesigning a course or curriculum? To justify the amount of time spent on a program or the new equipment needed for it?

2. *Determine what you need to know.*

   Who attended the program? Have the patrons had prior training using the library or the online catalog? Did the students get what they needed from the instruction?

3. *Determine whom to ask (the target audience).*

   Do you need to ask everyone or only a representative sample?

4. *Determine the best way to find out what you need.*

   Some sample methods follow.

   a) Select ten to fifteen questions to ask patrons online as they finish using the new online catalog.

   b) Select three questions that the circulation staff can ask patrons as they check out about . . . the new signs . . . the new remodeling . . . a new CD-ROM index.

   c) Select ten questions that volunteers could ask patrons as they leave, about . . . the children's program . . . the new information kiosk . . . the new CD-ROM.

---

3. Roberts, p. 48.

4. Janet Freedman, and Harold Bantly, "Techniques of Program Evaluation," in *Teaching Librarians to Teach: On-the-Job Training for Bibliographic Instruction Librarians* (Metuchen, N.J.: Scarecrow Press, 1986), p. 191.

5. Raya Fidel, "The Case Study Method: A Case Study," in *Qualitative Research in Information Management* (Englewood, Colo.: Libraries Unlimited, 1992), pp. 39–40.

d) Design a one-page evaluation of a librarian's presentation.

e) Choose eight questions that can be inserted into the gas company's bill mailing about . . . the library's hours . . . bookmobile service.

f) Choose twenty questions for a half-page insert in the local or campus newspaper or newsletter about library services or programs.

g) Design a survey to be sent to all faculty members about the need for new or existing instruction programs or knowledge of what already exists.

5. *Develop the questions.*

a) Select either nonstructured (open-ended) or structured (fixed response such as "yes–no" or multiple-choice) questions.

b) Determine what demographic data you need to know, such as age, year in school, or education.

c) Write the questions. Important elements in constructing evaluation questionnaires or surveys are addressed in the following section on "Developing the Questionnaire or Evaluation Form."

6. *Pretest the questions and revise them.*

This eliminates questions that are misinterpreted and yield irrelevant answers.

7. *Assemble the questionnaire.*

Layout is important! (See p. 5).

8. *Include a cover letter or introductory paragraph.*

This should explain why the questionnaire is being administered and approximately how long it will take to complete.

9. *Determine how and by whom the results will be tallied.*

How will they be used and/or disseminated? (See below, "Results of Evaluation," p. 6.)

10. *Report the results.*

(See below, "Results of Evaluation," p. 6.)

Surveys and evaluations produce valid information, not just impressions. They tell us what we do, how we do it, how well we do it, and what we need to do. Don't be afraid! With proper prior planning, you can create a product that will yield usable and useful results.

Developing the Questionnaire or Evaluation Form

Introducing the Form

Begin by telling the respondent why this evaluation is being undertaken. Guarantee confidentiality if this is important, or ask for a name and address or phone number if follow-up may be necessary. This can be accomplished through use of a cover letter or a clearly worded paragraph at the beginning. Provide instructions on how to complete the questionnaire. Do *not* depend solely on verbal instructions.

EXAMPLE

Please help us to evaluate this workshop by answering the questions below and adding your comments.

Writing the Questions

1. Begin with a few nonthreatening questions, such as demographic questions.[6]

2. Place important questions toward the beginning (but after demographic questions).

3. Group questions into logical coherent sections covering, for example, the materials, the instructor, and attitudes.

4. Avoid making the questionnaire seem like a test.

5. Be sure that all words are understood by the respondents. "Each question should be so clearly worded that all respondents will interpret it the same way." Don't use library jargon! A questionnaire should always be pretested to determine whether it is clear and appropriate to the audience.

---

6. The material presented here on writing questions and layout follows closely the advice of Douglas R. Berdie, John F. Anderson, and Marsha A. Niebuhr, *Questionnaires: Design and Use,* 2nd ed. (Metuchen, N.J.: Scarecrow Press, 1986).

6. Avoid emotionally charged language. Use non-sexist, nonracial language and avoid terms that suggest ethnic bias.

7. Use open-ended questions selectively. These may be useful for identifying noteworthy issues, but should be asked in small numbers or as a pretest (to determine appropriate choices for answers for the final version).

8. Attitudinal questions with a range of answers should always be written in the form of a statement.

9. Avoid double negatives.

10. Beware of using abbreviations.

11. Be sure that each question asks for only one piece of information. (Ask whether the handout was *clear* or whether it was *useful*, but NOT BOTH in the same question.)

12. Avoid vague terms such as "several"; "vague questions encourage vague answers."

Determining the Layout

Be sure to provide instructions with each question or set of questions, as appropriate. Some possibilities include:

- *Circle one answer for each question.*
- *Check all that apply.*
- *Fill in the blank.*
- *Fill in the appropriate responses on the attached computer answer sheet.*
- *Write your comments on the back of this sheet.*

Other samples are demonstrated in the examples given later in this section.

Here are a few hints to keep in mind in planning the layout of your evaluation form.

1. Make the form appealing to the eye.

2. Avoid the temptation to overcrowd the pages.

3. Make the form brief. Respondents quickly lose interest in long questionnaires.

4. Indicate clearly where the answers belong.

5. Give brief but clear instructions for completing the form.

6. Avoid using both sides of the page whenever possible.

7. Use boldface type to identify individual sections or emphasize words.

8. Print all instructions in boldface or italics.

9. Arrange responses vertically, not horizontally.

10. Choose one type of question for the main body (e.g., multiple choice or yes/no).

EXAMPLES

1. I use the <Blank> Library: (*Check one.*)

    ___ Daily
    ___ Weekly
    ___ Monthly
    ___ Once or twice a year
    ___ Never

2. The new library signs make it easier to find the children's section.   (*Circle one number.*)

    Strongly   Strongly
    agree   1   2   3   4   5   disagree

3. The handout on <blank> is easy to understand. (*Circle the number of your answer.*)

    1 Strongly agree
    2 Agree
    3 Neutral/Undecided
    4 Disagree
    5 Strongly disagree

    or

Use the following responses for questions 4–10 to indicate your feelings about our new CD-ROM databases. Fill in your responses on the attached computer answer sheet.

    1/A Strongly agree
    2/B Agree
    3/C Neutral/Undecided
    4/D Disagree
    5/E Strongly disagree

Note: When a computer answer sheet gives you answer choices such as 1/A, it is best to use this as your sample answer format.

---

4. The <blank> CD-ROM was easy to use.

5. The <blank> CD-ROM was available when I needed to use it.

Although using Likert or other attitudinal scales for survey questions appears scientific and objective, they require care in the wording of questions and statements and the construction of multiple-choice answers. For example, negative statements should be interspersed among positive ones to combat the "halo effect." Moreover, all scales should be balanced, with an equal number of options on either side of the middle. (See Appendix C for examples of attitudinal scales and additional information.)

Allow a final question or two for respondents to tell you about things you haven't asked, and to make comments.

EXAMPLE

If you have additional comments about the online catalog workshop, please write them in the space below.

Closing the Form

Thank respondents for taking the time to complete the survey or evaluation. If the form must be returned rather than completed on-site, be sure to include a complete address. Providing a self-addressed envelope or printing your address on the reverse side of a foldable form will help respondents to return the item to the right place.

EXAMPLES

Thank you for your cooperation in completing this questionnaire. Please return it to your <blank> teacher.

Thank you for completing this evaluation of <blank>. Please return it to:

> <Name>
> <Library>
> <Address>
> <City, State, Zip>

Results of Evaluation

Tabulating, Coding, and Analyzing the Results

Consider how the responses to your survey or evaluation form will be coded and tabulated or scored before administering it. As there are numerous methods for tabulating results, explore your options when planning the form, and choose the one that best meets your needs. The simplest method is to hand-tabulate the number of persons who respond in each way and calculate percentages. Many readily available software packages, such as Lotus or SPSS, provide more sophisticated analyses. Remember, however, that statistical programs can overanalyze the results to the point of meaninglessness. An excess of information only obfuscates an issue. Another approach is to seek help from an expert. Resource people available to you might include the testing service or statistical consultant at your college or university, the state or area education association for your school, the state library personnel for your public library, or an in-house specialist.

Reporting the Results

The purpose of doing a survey or evaluation is to make a point. Inform administrators or the public or user groups of the results of your efforts. State the implications clearly. If, however, the results are not as explicit as you had hoped, use the opportunity to explain what you learned and how it can improve future projects and instruction efforts.

Remember that surveys and evaluations are learning experiences. Use their results to make adjustments and improve your future endeavors.

Model Questions for Evaluation Instruments

Notes on Using These Questions

This handbook is designed as a guide for simplifying the process of planning and evaluating library instruction. Its sample questions and statements, derived from instruments used by libraries throughout the country, can in turn be used to design a wide variety of new instruments. These samples are arranged in fourteen sections proceeding from introducing the evaluation form to the closing "thank you." In between come sections on evaluating materials, facilities, assignments, methods, instructors, and much more. Each section commences with an explanation of the types of questions it contains, and the rationale for using them.

Users of this handbook should note the following:

Many similar questions appear in various sections (or within the same section) in different forms and formats. Choose the versions that apply to your particular situation, or that otherwise work best for you.

Commentary about individual questions or statements appears in italics and is set off by rules above and below.

The designation <blank> in questions or statements indicates that you must fill in the institution, library, subject, course, program, or tool specific to your situation.

The underlining of words in questions or statements is intended to add emphasis or clarity.

A few sample statements have been stated in the negative to avoid the "halo effect" that can result when respondents see only positive statements and therefore tend to be overly positive in their responses. Other statements can be recast negatively at your discretion.

Questions may be adapted for instruments to be used before, during, or after instruction.

Additional information about tabulating responses is provided in the Introduction, under the heading, "Results of Evaluation." Sample scales are shown in Appendix B, and sample questionnaires are provided in Appendix D.

SECTION 1
Sample Introductory Statements

Your evaluation or questionnaire should always begin with an explanation of why it is being conducted and how the responses will be used. A short statement covering these points will improve the response/return rate. It should also guarantee confidentiality if this is important to the respondents. This can be done through a cover letter or a short paragraph at the top of the form itself.

A cover letter is essential in a mailed survey or evaluation. It should be short and to the point. Because your cover letter gives the first impression, it should be attractive to the eye. Your library's letterhead stationery adds legitimacy to your request for information, as does the signature of an authority figure.

A cover letter should address the following questions:

Why is this evaluation being done?

Who is being surveyed?

What is the approximate time required for completion?

What is the deadline for returning the responses?

Where should the questionnaire be returned, and to whom?

Will a follow-up be conducted if the original form is not returned?

The introduction to your evaluation form should contain clear, concise directions for answering the questions. Vaguely written or spoken explanations often lead to misunderstandings and uneven responses. *Do not* leave the explanations to chance! Test your survey with a small group first, and rectify ambiguities for the final product. Keep in mind that many people read only the first sentence of the introduction, and some do not read directions at all. You may wish to highlight instructions by setting them in boldface or italic type.

Suggested Reading

Berdie, Douglas R., et al. *Questionnaires: Design and Use.* 2nd ed. Metuchen, N.J.: Scarecrow Press, 1986. Pages 51–53.

EXAMPLES OF INTRODUCTORY STATEMENTS

The <Blank> Library wishes to determine our patrons' satisfaction with our new online catalog. Please return this survey to <Blank> by <date>.

The Instruction Department of the <Blank> Library wishes to evaluate our graduate student orientation session on <blank> to better serve the research needs of new graduate students.

The Instruction Department of the <Blank> Library would appreciate knowing your feelings about the library research skills of incoming freshman students at <Blank>.

OUTLINE OF SECTION 1

Sample Introductory Statements

I. General Introductions

II. Introductions for Evaluative Questionnaires

III. Introduction for Open-Ended Questionnaires

I. General Introductions

1.
STUDENT FEEDBACK SHEET

Librarian's Name: _____ Date: _____

Course Title: _____

Please help us by taking a few moments to complete this evaluation form. All comments are welcome.

2.
SUBJECT SESSION EVALUATION

Class: _____ Librarian Instructor: _____

Please CIRCLE the appropriate responses for each question:

or

Please FILL IN the appropriate circles on the attached answer sheet.

3. *Please answer the following questions designed to assess your knowledge of how to use the <Blank> Library to do research.*

4. *You can help us to find out if we succeeded in teaching you how to find magazine articles in the <Blank> School Media Center by answering the following questions. Please mark your answers in the boxes next to the questions.*

5. *We would appreciate it if you would answer the following questions designed to assess the effectiveness of our Internet training.*

II. Introductions for Evaluative Questionnaires

1. Evaluation

Please take a few minutes to answer the following questions. Your responses will be used to improve our instruction. Please write comments, especially if you have answered "no" to any of the questions. Thank you.

2. **Library Session Evaluation**

Please take a few minutes to tell us whether the library session you had in <blank> was helpful. We appreciate your feedback—it will help us to do a better job.

3. *Please help us to evaluate this class by answering the questions below and writing your comments.*

4. *The purpose of this questionnaire is to learn your opinions about the class you just attended. Indicate your opinions on the questionnaire by filling in your response to each question using the following scale.*

   1   if you Strongly agree
   2   if you Agree
   3   if you are Neutral or Undecided
   4   if you Disagree
   5   if you Strongly disagree

5. *This questionnaire asks you to evaluate how well we succeeded in training you to use our online catalog. Please give us your opinion by answering the following questions on the attached answer sheet.*

6. *We would like to determine if we answered your questions in our tour of the <Blank> Media Center. Please take the time to let us know if our orientation was helpful to you. Leave the form in the box on the librarians' desk.*

7. *Please help us in determining if our <Blank> CD-ROM training session was helpful to your students in completing their research assignment.*

III. Introduction for Open-Ended Questionnaires

1. *This evaluation form is designed to produce information about our instruction that will make it easier to determine what, if any, changes need to be made. Your thoughtful and complete response will be most appreciated. Responses that include specific examples and illustrations will provide the most useful data. You need not sign the form. Please return it at the next class session or any time during the next two days to <Blank>. Thank you.*

SECTION 2
Demographics/Patron Information

The information provided in this section will help programmers/instructors in targeting the level of instruction for the intended audience. Understanding your audience is key to interpreting results of surveys or evaluations.

Select those questions that will allow you to identify your audience. This handbook may not cover all factors that are important to your survey or evaluation. Its examples should, however, help you to determine who your intended audience includes. Once you have determined whom your respondents will be, pretest your questionnaire to be sure that the questions elicit the type of responses you intend. Identify your audience correctly. Ask only those questions that yield information you need for your data analysis; for example, questions about age and sex are not always appropriate. Ask questions about grade point average only if they will help you with your analysis; this type of question could offend some potential respondents but might be necessary for surveys that attempt to predict outcomes such as success in college based on the ability to do research.

Demographic questions can be placed at the beginning or the end of the questionnaire. In evaluations of current programs, demographics usually precede the evaluative questions; in needs assessments or surveys, however, they often appear last so that respondents who don't wish to give this type of information will not refuse to answer the other questions as well.

Suggested Readings

Van House, Nancy A., et al. *Output Measures for Public Libraries: A Manual of Standardization Procedures.* 2nd ed. Chicago: American Library Association, 1987.

Walter, Virginia A. *Output Measures for Public Library Service to Children: A Manual of Standardization Procedures.* Chicago: American Library Association, 1992.

OUTLINE OF SECTION 2

Demographics/Patron Information

I. Age

II. Sex

III. Race

IV. Level of Education

V. Grade Level/Classification

VI. Major

VII. Grade Point Average

I. Age

If this information is important the categories should be adjusted to match your audience. Try to make the increments of equal size and leave room on the top and bottom for persons whose responses don't match the groupings.

1. Age: (*Please list.*) _____

2. How old are you? _____

3. Age:

Below are some possible categories:

a)	16–18		a)	5–7
b)	19–21	*or*	b)	8–10
c)	22–24		c)	11–13
d)	25–27		
e)	over 27		

4. Age: (*Please check one.*)

___ Under 25
___ 26–35
___ 36–45   *or*
___ 46–55
___ 56–65
___ Over 65

___ under 14
___ 14–15
___ 16–17
___ 18 or older

II. Sex

1. Sex:

___ Female
___ Male

or

a. male
b. female

2. Sex:

    [   ] F

    [   ] M

3. Are you a boy or a girl?   (*Circle the right answer.*)

    BOY   GIRL

III. Race

In this type of question, choices of responses should reflect your population.

---

1. Race:

    a. Caucasian

    b. Afro-American

    c. Hispanic

    d. Asian

    e. Other, please identify: _____

IV. Level of Education

1. Level of education:

    a. Less than a high school education

    b. High school or GED

    c. Some college

    d. 4-year college degree

    e. Advanced degree

V. Grade Level/Classification

1. What is your present grade level? (*Circle your answer.*)

    a. 1st grade

    b. 2nd grade

    c. 3rd grade

    d. 4th grade

    e. 5th grade

    f. 6th grade

    g. 7th grade

    h. 8th grade

2. What is your grade level or class level?

___ freshman		a. freshman
___ sophomore	*or*	b. sophomore
___ junior		c. junior
___ senior		d. senior
		e. special student or other

3. Status: (*Check one.*)

    ___ Freshman

    ___ Sophomore

    ___ Junior

    ___ Senior

    ___ Other, please specify: _____

4. Class level: (*Check one.*)

    ___ Graduate

    ___ Undergraduate

    ___ Other

5. Please check Class:

  ___ Freshman

  ___ Sophomore

  ___ Junior

  ___ Senior

  ___ Master's

  ___ Doctorate

 and Status: (*Check all that apply.*)

  ___ New student

  ___ Transfer student

  ___ Returning student

  ___ International student

  ___ Special student

  ___ Part-time student

  ___ Full-time student

6. Status: (*Check one.*)

  ___ Undergraduate

  ___ Graduate

  ___ Staff

  ___ Faculty

  ___ Other—please specify _____

 Department: _____

7. Status: (*Circle one.*)

  1 Researcher

  2 Staff member

  3 Administrator

  4 Visitor

  5 Other, please specify _____

8. How many years have you attended <Blank>?

  ___ Less than one

  ___ One

  ___ Two

  ___ Three or more

9. Number of college courses you have previously taken:

      ( ) 0–5
      ( ) 6–10
      ( ) 11–15
      ( ) 15+
      ( ) Already have a degree: A.A., B.A., M.A. *(Circle one.)*
      Other _____

10. Number of college credits already completed:

    1   none
    2   fewer than 15
    3   16 to 30
    4   31 to 45
    5   46 or more

These categories may vary but should be of equal size.

11. Number of quarters/semesters you have *completed* at <Blank>: *(Count summer school as one.)*

    ___ a)   None
    ___ b)   One
    ___ c)   Two
    ___ d)   Three
    ___ e)   More than three

12. Please indicate your student status.

    [ ] A   Full-time day
    [ ] B   Part-time day
    [ ] C   Evening
    [ ] D   Saturday only
    [ ] E   Other. Please explain.

13. Did you transfer here?

    ___ Did not transfer here
    ___ Transferred from a two-year college
    ___ Transferred from another four-year college

14. How long have you been out of high school?

    [ ] A   Less than one year

    [ ] B   1–5 years

    [ ] C   6–10 years

    [ ] D   More than 10 years

15. Number of students in your high school graduating class:

___ a)	1–250			1	1–50
___ b)	251–500	*or*		2	51–100
___ c)	501–750			3	101–150
___ d)	751–1000			4	151–200
___ e)	Over 1000			5	201–250
				6	over 250

VI. Major

1. Department or major: _____

2. Is this session in your major field?

    ___ Yes

    ___ No

3. Is this course required for graduation?

    ___ Yes

    ___ No

4. Please indicate your major by checking one of these categories:

    [ ] <Business>

    [ ] <Science and Related Technologies>

    [ ] <Humanities>

    [ ] <Social Sciences>

    [ ] Undeclared

VII. Grade Point Average

1. What was your overall grade point average at the completion of last semester?   (*Circle one.*)

    a)   2.0 or below

    b)   2.1–2.5

    c)   2.6–3.0

    d)   3.1–3.5

    e)   3.6 or above

    f)   new student

2. What is your approximate cumulative grade point average?   (*Check one.*)

    ( ) 3.50–4.00

    ( ) 3.00–3.49

    ( ) 2.50–2.99

    ( ) 2.00–2.49

    ( ) Under 2.00

Although many of the examples in this section are most applicable to academic libraries, they can be adapted for other library settings.

SECTION 3
Patrons' Library Background

The information in this section will help you to assess the knowledge and library expertise of your clientele. This assessment will enable you to target specific areas of need in preparing an instruction session. You may want to conduct this type of survey well before the session or class. Copies could, for example, be sent to students or to their teacher. The responses will provide a useful planning tool.

Decide if you need to define terms (e.g., periodical, online catalog) before you ask your questions. Then select the types of questions most pertinent to your library setting. In questions that ask about frequency of library use, terms such as "frequently" or "seldom" are best avoided, as they are open to personal interpretation; instead use specific time periods, such as "once a day," "once a week," or "once a month."

What you decide to ask may depend on the audience. Surveys about previous library use or surveys requesting teachers' perceptions of their students' library use are often important in deciding on the type of instruction. Such surveys are commonly done in tan-

dem to determine both the similarity of responses and where the gaps exist between real library experiences and teachers' perceptions of the same. Surveys of faculty/teacher perceptions of student ability can be eye-opening experiences for librarians, as faculty expectations of students are often unrealistically high.

Suggested Readings

Haws, Rae, Lorna Peterson, and Diana Shonrock. "Survey of Faculty Attitudes towards a Basic Library Skills Course." *College & Research Libraries News* 50 (March 1989): 201–3.

Lester, Linda. "Faculty Perceptions of Students' Knowledge and Use of Libraries." Charlottesville: University of Virginia, Alderman Library, 1984. ERIC ED 247949. 46 pp.

Rice, James, Jr. *Teaching Library Use: A Guide for Library Instruction.* Westport, Conn.: Greenwood Press, 1981. Pages 97–129.

OUTLINE OF SECTION 3

Patrons' Library Background

I. Library Usage

II. Previous Library Usage

III. Previous Library Instruction

IV. Faculty/Teacher Perception of Students' Skills

I. Library Usage

1. I use the library: (*Check one.*)

___ Daily

___ Weekly

___ Monthly

___ Once or twice per year

___ Never

2. How often do you use <Blank> Library?

___ at least once a week

___ at least twice a month

___ less than twice a month

___ never

3. I use the bookmobile: (*Check one.*)

___ at least once a week

___ at least once a month

___ once or twice per year

___ never

4. Check the type of library that you use most often:

___ a) school library

___ b) college or university library

___ c) public library

___ d) other (what type?) _____

5. In general, how often have your courses required papers or research projects involving use of the library?

___ at least once a month

___ at least twice a semester

___ less than twice a semester

___ never

6. How often do you use the <Blank> Library for each of the following purposes? Check one response in each category below.

    a) To study for courses.

        ____ at least once a week

        ____ at least twice a month

        ____ less than twice a month

        ____ never

    b) To use reserve materials for courses.

        ____ at least once a week

        ____ at least twice a month

        ____ less than twice a month

        ____ never

    c) To obtain information for research and/or class assignments.

        ____ at least once a week

        ____ at least twice a month

        ____ less than twice a month

        ____ never

    d) For non-class-related reading.

        ____ at least once a week

        ____ at least twice a month

        ____ less than twice a month

        ____ never

    e) To use periodicals (magazines, journals, newspapers).

        ____ at least once a week

        ____ at least twice a month

        ____ less than twice a month

        ____ never

    f) To socialize or relax.

        ____ at least once a week

        ____ at least twice a month

        ____ less than twice a month

        ____ never

    g) For what other purpose do you regularly use <Blank> Library?   (*Please specify.*)

II. Previous Library Usage

1. How often did you use a library in your studies before you came to <Blank>?

    a) Not at all
    b) 1 to 3 times a month
    c) 4 to 6 times a month
    d) More than 6 times a month

2. Have you used other <academic/public/school> libraries before?

    ___ Yes
    ___ No

3. Please indicate the type and extent of use you have made of this library prior to this instruction session.

    ___ Never used the library before
    ___ Used for courses in the same discipline
    ___ Used for courses in other disciplines

4. Please make a check mark in front of the library activities you took part in this <semester, summer, etc.>.

    ___ Worked on a class assignment
    ___ Did homework
    ___ Studied with friends
    ___ Asked for help with a paper
    ___ Read a book
    ___ Other, please list _____

5. Please indicate the type and extent of use you have made of other <school libraries, media centers, public libraries> prior to this library session.

    ___ Not at all
    ___ 1 to 3 times a month
    ___ 4 to 6 times a month
    ___ More than 6 times a month

6. Have you ever used a CD-ROM database to find articles on a subject?

    ___ Yes

    ___ No

    ___ Don't know

7. Have you ever asked for assistance at the reference desk?

    ___ Yes

    ___ No

III. Previous Library Instruction

1. Have you ever had library instruction at <Blank> before?

    ___ Yes

    ___ No

    If yes, please list course name(s) and number(s):

2. This is my first session relating to <blank area> at <Blank> Library:

    ___ Yes

    ___ No

3. Before taking this course when did anyone explain how to use library resources to you? Check all that apply.

    ___ In grade school

    ___ In high school from a librarian

    ___ In high school from a teacher

    ___ In the public library from a librarian

    ___ Never

    ___ Other, please identify

4. Before taking this course, what kinds of instruction in using the \<Blank\> Library had you had?

    ___ a) None

    ___ b) Orientation to Library by a library staff member

    ___ c) Guided tour of \<Blank\> Library

    ___ d) Instruction from a librarian

    ___ e) Instruction from an instructor teaching in one of your classes

    ___ f) Assistance at Reference Desk

5. My previous library training includes: *(Check as many of these as seem appropriate to your situation.)*

    ___ a) How to use a card catalog

    ___ b) How to use reference books (encyclopedias, dictionaries, etc.)

    ___ c) How to use *Readers' Guide to Periodical Literature*

    ___ d) How to use the Dewey Decimal System

    ___ e) How to use the Library of Congress System

    ___ f) How to use periodical indexes (other than *Readers' Guide*)

    ___ g) How to use an online catalog

    ___ h) How to use the Internet

    ___ i) How to use CD-ROM indexes, e.g., \<Blank\>

    ___ j) Online or paid computer searches: BRS, DIALOG, CIP, etc.

6. Which of the following did you know how to use before the class session on research in the library? *(Check all that apply.)*

    ___ Card catalog

    ___ CD-ROM periodical and newspaper indexes

    ___ Print indexes

    ___ Subject encyclopedia or dictionary

    ___ Specialized bibliography

    ___ Online catalog

7. In using the library for this course or other courses at <Blank>, what areas have you had problems with?   (*Check all that apply.*)

    ___ Choosing and narrowing a topic for a research paper

    ___ Finding background materials in an encyclopedia, etc.

    ___ Finding appropriate subject headings and using the <card catalog/online catalog> to find books on a topic

    ___ Using periodical indexes

    ___ Finding books related to your topic that were not already checked out

    ___ Finding citations to books and journals that the library does not own

    ___ Other:

IV. Faculty/Teacher Perception of Students' Skills

1. Incoming freshmen do <u>not</u> have the necessary skills to use a research library.

    1   Strongly agree

    2   Agree

    3   Neutral/Undecided

    4   Disagree

    5   Strongly disagree

2. It is important for students to know how to use the library.

    1   Strongly agree

    2   Agree

    3   Neutral/Undecided

    4   Disagree

    5   Strongly disagree

3. Having the library staff teach basic library skills relieves me of having to teach research skills.

    1   Strongly agree

    2   Agree

    3   Neutral/Undecided

    4   Disagree

    5   Strongly disagree

4. A basic library skills course establishes the foundation for learning discipline-specific research skills.

    1   Strongly agree

    2   Agree

    3   Neutral/Undecided

    4   Disagree

    5   Strongly disagree

5. A basic library skills course should be taught at <Blank>.

    1   Strongly agree

    2   Agree

    3   Neutral/Undecided

    4   Disagree

    5   Strongly disagree

6. I feel that my students were adequately prepared to do <blank> level research.

    1   Strongly agree

    2   Agree

    3   Neutral/Undecided

    4   Disagree

    5   Strongly disagree

7. Do you feel that your freshman students received adequate preparation in high school to use the <Blank> Library?

    ___ Yes

    ___ No

    ___ Not sure

8. Was this the first time you have used the library's instruction services?

    ___ Yes

    ___ No

If no, on how many previous occasions have you used these services? _____

9. How would you rate your students' ability to use the library? *(Circle one.)*

   High 1 2 3 4 5 Low

10. How many times in the past have you planned lessons with a librarian?

    ___ Never
    ___ 1–2
    ___ 3–5
    ___ 6–10
    ___ More than 10

11. Are there things about college students in general, or this class in particular, that would be helpful for the librarian to know?

SECTION 4
Physical Facilities

Evaluation of library facilities, concerning either the actual placement and arrangement of library services and resources or the classroom in which instruction takes place, is not widely practiced. Yet the environment in which patrons use and learn about resources can significantly affect feelings of library anxiety. In all types of libraries, clear and instructive signs and logically arranged service points will help patrons to feel more comfortable. Similarly, a training facility that has good acoustics and lighting and where on-screen projections are easy to read will enhance patrons' learning experiences. Mastering complex library resources can be stressful enough without impediments such as distracting noises or poor visibility. Elements to be considered when evaluating physical facilities include acoustics, temperature, lighting, and accessibility as well as the overall ambiance of the space.

Suggested Readings

Feinman, Valerie J. "Library Instruction: What Is Our Classroom?" *Computers in Libraries* 14 (February 1994): 33–36.

Kusack, James M. "Facility Evaluation in Libraries: A Strategy and Methodology for Managers." *Library Administration and Management* 7 (Spring 1993): 107–11.

Roberts, Anne F., and Susan G. Blandy. *Public Relations for Librarians.* Englewood, Colo.: Libraries Unlimited, 1989. Pages 56–63.

Westbrook, Lynn, and Sharon DeDecker. "Supporting User Needs and Skills to Minimize Library Anxiety: Considerations for Academic Libraries." *Reference Librarian* 40 (1993): 43–51.

OUTLINE OF SECTION 4

Physical Facilities

I. Library Facilities

II. Classroom/Lab Facilities

I. Library Facilities

1. The open hours of the library are convenient for me.

   1 Strongly agree
   2 Agree
   3 Neutral/Undecided
   4 Disagree
   5 Strongly disagree

2. The open hours of the Reference Desk are adequate for my needs.

   1 Strongly agree
   2 Agree
   3 Neutral/Undecided
   4 Disagree
   5 Strongly disagree

3. The environment (acoustics, temperature, lighting, etc.) was a good one for learning.

   1 Strongly agree
   2 Agree
   3 Neutral/Undecided
   4 Disagree
   5 Strongly disagree

4. The level of noise in the library inhibited my ability to study.

   1 Strongly agree
   2 Agree
   3 Neutral/Undecided
   4 Disagree
   5 Strongly disagree

5. The temperature in the library was too warm for studying.

   1 Strongly agree
   2 Agree
   3 Neutral/Undecided
   4 Disagree
   5 Strongly disagree

6. The atmosphere in the library is conducive to student learning.

    1   Strongly agree

    2   Agree

    3   Neutral/Undecided

    4   Disagree

    5   Strongly disagree

7. The check-out procedures are convenient.

    1   Strongly agree

    2   Agree

    3   Neutral/Undecided

    4   Disagree

    5   Strongly disagree

8. There are enough tables and chairs in the study areas.

    1   Strongly agree

    2   Agree

    3   Neutral/Undecided

    4   Disagree

    5   Strongly disagree

9. The special areas of the Reference Room are clearly marked.

    1   Strongly agree

    2   Agree

    3   Neutral/Undecided

    4   Disagree

    5   Strongly disagree

10. There are enough CD-ROM workstations available.

    1   Strongly agree

    2   Agree

    3   Neutral/Undecided

    4   Disagree

    5   Strongly disagree

11. Did you find the signs in the library helpful?

    ___ Yes

    ___ No

    ___ Didn't notice any signs

12. Do you have suggestions about how the arrangement of the library or the location of its services might be improved?

13. Do you have comments concerning improvements in services or physical layout of the library?

14. Changes in the site, physical facilities, scheduling, projection visibility, etc., that I would recommend are:

15. Do you have suggestions for improving the signs in the library?

II. Classroom/Lab Facilities

1. The lighting in the classroom was adequate for note taking.

    1   Strongly agree

    2   Agree

    3   Neutral/Undecided

    4   Disagree

    5   Strongly disagree

2. The arrangement of the classroom helped make discussion possible.

    1   Strongly agree

    2   Agree

    3   Neutral/Undecided

    4   Disagree

    5   Strongly disagree

3. There were enough seats in the classroom.

    1   Strongly agree

    2   Agree

    3   Neutral/Undecided

    4   Disagree

    5   Strongly disagree

4. There were <u>not</u> enough computers in the computer lab.

    1   Strongly agree

    2   Agree

    3   Neutral/Undecided

    4   Disagree

    5   Strongly disagree

5. The <blank> equipment was helpful to my understanding of the material presented.

    1   Strongly agree

    2   Agree

    3   Neutral/Undecided

    4   Disagree

    5   Strongly disagree

6. The computers in the teaching facility were in good working order.

    1   Strongly agree

    2   Agree

    3   Neutral/Undecided

    4   Disagree

    5   Strongly disagree

7. The computers in the teaching facility were easy to use.

    1   Strongly agree

    2   Agree

    3   Neutral/Undecided

    4   Disagree

    5   Strongly disagree

8. The arrangement of the classroom/lab was: (*Check one.*)

    poor   fair   good   very good   excellent

    [   ]   [   ]   [   ]   [   ]   [   ]

9. The visibility of the on-screen projection in the classroom was:

    ___ excellent

    ___ very good

    ___ good

    ___ fair

    ___ poor

SECTION 5
Materials

Printed resources in the form of textbooks, handouts, workbooks, assignments, and pathfinders used during library instruction are an important component of the learning process. Handouts and other printed sources serve multiple instructional purposes: they can reinforce the content of the library presentation or supplement the library presentation with additional information. Printed assignments provide students with an opportunity to get hands-on experience using library resources; materials such as pathfinders or bibliographies list resources that individuals can consult independently. In some cases, handouts and workbooks are the only way that patrons learn about the library and its resources. When evaluating library materials, keep in mind that handouts and other library materials should be well organized and easy to read as well as useful and relevant to the library presentation or research assignment.

Suggested Readings

Peterson, Lorna, and Jamie W. Coniglio. "Readability of Selected Academic Library Guides." *RQ* (Winter 1987): 233–39.

Roberts, Anne F., and Susan G. Blandy. "Choosing Formats." In *Library Instruction for Librarians*. 2nd rev. ed. Englewood, Colo.: Libraries Unlimited, 1989.

OUTLINE OF SECTION 5

Materials

I.   Textbooks, Manuals, or Workbooks

    A.   Students

    B.   Teachers/Instructors

II. Handouts, Bibliographies, or Pathfinders

I. Textbooks, Manuals, or Workbooks

A. Students

1. The workbook was a very useful tool for learning about the library.

    1   Strongly agree

    2   Agree

    3   Neutral/Undecided

    4   Disagree

    5   Strongly disagree

2. I needed additional individual assistance to complete the workbook.

    1   Strongly agree

    2   Agree

    3   Neutral/Undecided

    4   Disagree

    5   Strongly disagree

3. The textbook was helpful to my understanding of the session.

    1   Strongly agree

    2   Agree

    3   Neutral/Undecided

    4   Disagree

    5   Strongly disagree

4. The information in the manual was useful.

    1   Strongly agree

    2   Agree

    3   Neutral/Undecided

    4   Disagree

    5   Strongly disagree

5. The manual provided a good explanation of the library research process.

    1   Strongly agree

    2   Agree

    3   Neutral/Undecided

    4   Disagree

    5   Strongly disagree

6. I liked the self-paced nature of the workbook.

    1   Strongly agree

    2   Agree

    3   Neutral/Undecided

    4   Disagree

    5   Strongly disagree

7. The concepts presented in the text were adequately covered in class.

    1   Strongly agree

    2   Agree

    3   Neutral/Undecided

    4   Disagree

    5   Strongly disagree

8. The computer tutorials helped me to complete the work in the manual.

    1   Strongly agree

    2   Agree

    3   Neutral/Undecided

    4   Disagree

    5   Strongly disagree

9. The search strategy work sheet served as a useful tool for helping to locate materials.

    1   Strongly agree

    2   Agree

    3   Neutral/Undecided

    4   Disagree

    5   Strongly disagree

10. a) What did you find to be most helpful about the workbook?

b) What was least helpful?

11. Please comment on the textbook or major readings used for this session. (Were readings appropriate, too hard, too easy? Was the amount of reading appropriate? Did the reading help to meet course objectives?)

12. If there were words in the textbook or handouts and/or directions that you found hard to understand, please list them here. (Use the back of this page if you need more space.)

13. How effective were each of the following in achieving the course's goals? (*Check one space in each row.*)

	Very effective	Somewhat effective	Neutral	Somewhat ineffective	Very ineffective	Not applicable
Texts	_____	_____	_____	_____	_____	_____
Other readings	_____	_____	_____	_____	_____	_____
Lab instructor (note if TA)	_____	_____	_____	_____	_____	_____

B. Teachers/Instructors

1. Was the textbook required for your students?

___ Yes ___ No

2. a) Did your students use the text?

___ Yes ___ No ___ Text, but not exercises

b) If your answer is "no," what are you using as an alternative text or aid for teaching library usage?

3. If you used this text, which sections did you assign for reading?

___ Section 1

___ Section 2

___ Section 3

___ Section 4

___ Section 5

___ Selected portions of sections (Please identify.)

4. **a)** Do you plan to use this text when you next teach this course?

___ Yes ___ No (Explain below.)

b) If you are planning to use this text again, will you use it the same way that you used it this semester?

___ Yes

___ No (Please describe how your approach will differ.)

5. Does the text provide enough information about the use of libraries for the objectives of this course?

___ Provides enough for independent learning

___ Needs to provide more explanation or illustrations

___ Needs to include more resources

___ Provides too much information

___ Provides a base for classroom discussion and practice

6. Did any of your students have difficulty relating concepts presented in the text to practice in libraries?

___ All students

___ Most students

___ A few students

___ No students

II. Handouts, Bibliographies, or Pathfinders

1. The handouts listing the titles and call numbers of books to be described were helpful.

1 Strongly agree
2 Agree
3 Neutral/Undecided
4 Disagree
5 Strongly disagree

2. Guides and materials distributed were helpful.

1 Strongly agree
2 Agree
3 Neutral/Undecided
4 Disagree
5 Strongly disagree

3. The print materials given out by the librarian were useful.

1 Strongly agree
2 Agree
3 Neutral/Undecided
4 Disagree
5 Strongly disagree

4. The handouts helped to illustrate the lecture material.

1 Strongly agree
2 Agree
3 Neutral/Undecided
4 Disagree
5 Strongly disagree

5. The handouts that provided supplementary information not covered in the lecture will be useful.

1 Strongly agree
2 Agree
3 Neutral/Undecided
4 Disagree
5 Strongly disagree

6. The library instruction handouts my students received in class were useful for preparing their term papers.

    1   Strongly agree

    2   Agree

    3   Neutral/Undecided

    4   Disagree

    5   Strongly disagree

7. The handouts were <u>not</u> necessary.

    1   Strongly agree

    2   Agree

    3   Neutral/Undecided

    4   Disagree

    5   Strongly disagree

8. The number of handouts was appropriate for the instruction.

    1   Strongly agree

    2   Agree

    3   Neutral/Undecided

    4   Disagree

    5   Strongly disagree

9. The handouts present information in an accurate, organized, and understandable manner.

    1   Strongly agree

    2   Agree

    3   Neutral/Undecided

    4   Disagree

    5   Strongly disagree

10. The sample materials on <topic> were helpful.

    1   Strongly agree

    2   Agree

    3   Neutral/Undecided

    4   Disagree

    5   Strongly disagree

11. Handouts helped to <u>focus</u> and <u>highlight</u> the main points of the library presentation.

    1   Strongly agree

    2   Agree

    3   Neutral/Undecided

    4   Disagree

    5   Strongly disagree

12. Printed handouts were available for all information covered in the library presentation.

    1   Strongly agree

    2   Agree

    3   Neutral/Undecided

    4   Disagree

    5   Strongly disagree

13. The sources listed in the bibliographies were generally relevant.

    1   Strongly agree

    2   Agree

    3   Neutral/Undecided

    4   Disagree

    5   Strongly disagree

14. The bibliography will be useful for successfully completing my research project.

    1   Strongly agree

    2   Agree

    3   Neutral/Undecided

    4   Disagree

    5   Strongly disagree

15. The bibliographies were confusing.

    1   Strongly agree

    2   Agree

    3   Neutral/Undecided

    4   Disagree

    5   Strongly disagree

16. The printed materials I was given will be helpful for my research.

    1   Strongly agree

    2   Agree

    3   Neutral/Undecided

    4   Disagree

    5   Strongly disagree

17. The overall quality of instructional materials (handouts, overheads, etc.) was:

    ___ excellent

    ___ very good

    ___ good

    ___ fair

    ___ poor

18. Would additional handouts have been helpful?

    ___ No (Handouts were adequate.)

    ___ Yes (If so, describe the kinds of handouts you would like to have.)

19. What might we do to improve the handout(s)?

20. What do you think could have been added to the handouts to make them more useful?

21. What do you think could have been omitted from the handouts?

SECTION 6
Supporting Materials

Supporting materials include visual aids and other non-print instructional material used in library presentations. Videotapes, slides, transparencies, presentation software such as PowerPoint and Persuasion, computer-assisted instruction (CAI) such as Research Assistant, and computer projections and student computer workstations are all examples of instructional technology. In the increasingly electronic library environment, instructional technology has become critical for effective teaching.

When evaluating the technology and other instructional support material intended for bibliographic instruction, be sure to focus on its instructional effectiveness and relevance, rather than on the medium itself. Keep in mind that high-tech instructional methods such as videotapes and presentation software can be used to teach seemingly low-tech library skills such as developing a search strategy or using a print index. Similarly, low-tech materials such as overhead transparencies or even chalkboards can be an effective means for training individuals to use high-tech resources like online catalogs, CD-ROM indexes, and the Internet. Other elements to consider when evaluating instructional support materials include clarity, helpfulness, and appropriateness for the intended audience.

Suggested Readings

Anderson, James. "Using Projectors." *ECC News* (January 1990): 25–30.

Jacobson, Gertrude N., and Michael J. Albright. "Motivation Via Videotape: Key to Undergraduate Library Instruction in the Research Library." *Journal of Academic Librarianship* 9 (November 1983): 270–75.

Macakanja, Richard. "Creating Visual Presentation Materials." *ECC News* (January 1990): 24–25.

Puryear, Dorothy. "Computer-Aided Instruction for Literacy in Libraries." *Catholic Library World* 64 (October–March 1993–94): 40–42.

OUTLINE OF SECTION 6

Supporting Materials

I.   Visual Aids

II. Slides/Transparencies

III. Videotapes

IV. Demonstrations of Electronic Resources

V.   Computer-Aided Instruction (CAI)

I. Visual Aids

1. The visual aids were effective in explaining <blank>.

   1 Strongly agree
   2 Agree
   3 Neutral/Undecided
   4 Disagree
   5 Strongly disagree

2. Audiovisual materials (transparencies, slides, computer displays, etc.) were used effectively.

   1 Strongly agree
   2 Agree
   3 Neutral/Undecided
   4 Disagree
   5 Strongly disagree

3. Online demonstrations conducted during the library presentation helped to <u>focus</u> and <u>highlight</u> the main points of the presentation.

   1 Strongly agree
   2 Agree
   3 Neutral/Undecided
   4 Disagree
   5 Strongly disagree

4. Online demonstrations that supplemented the library presentation helped to <u>focus</u> and <u>highlight</u> the main points of the presentation.

   1 Strongly agree
   2 Agree
   3 Neutral/Undecided
   4 Disagree
   5 Strongly disagree

5. The library presentation helped me to learn the material presented in the workbook.

   1   Strongly agree
   2   Agree
   3   Neutral/Undecided
   4   Disagree
   5   Strongly disagree

6. The audiovisual aids (slides, transparencies, catalog projection) helped me to understand the presentation.

   1   Strongly agree
   2   Agree
   3   Neutral/Undecided
   4   Disagree
   5   Strongly disagree

7. Visual aids were useful supplements to the class.

   1   Strongly agree
   2   Agree
   3   Neutral/Undecided
   4   Disagree
   5   Strongly disagree

8. Visual aids were clear and easy to read.

   1   Strongly agree
   2   Agree
   3   Neutral/Undecided
   4   Disagree
   5   Strongly disagree

9. Audiovisual materials, teaching aids, demonstrations, or nonlecture teaching strategies were effective.

   1   Strongly agree
   2   Agree
   3   Neutral/Undecided
   4   Disagree
   5   Strongly disagree

10. Transparencies, screen projections, and audiovisuals helped to <u>focus</u> and <u>highlight</u> the main points of the library presentation.

    1   Strongly agree

    2   Agree

    3   Neutral/Undecided

    4   Disagree

    5   Strongly disagree

11. Transparencies, screen projections, and audiovisuals used during the library presentation were <u>large enough</u> to be <u>readable</u> by all participants.

    1   Strongly agree

    2   Agree

    3   Neutral/Undecided

    4   Disagree

    5   Strongly disagree

12. How would you rate the visual aids (slides, transparencies, computer demonstrations, etc.) used in this workshop?

    1   Excellent

    2   Very good

    3   Good

    4   Fair

    5   Poor

13. How often did your assignments in this class involve using nonprint library resources (records, filmstrips, computer disks, microfilm, videotapes)?

    1   Never

    2   1–2 times

    3   3–4 times

    4   5–6 times

    5   More than 6 times

II. Slides/Transparencies

1. The transparencies helped to illustrate the lecture material.

   1 Strongly agree
   2 Agree
   3 Neutral/Undecided
   4 Disagree
   5 Strongly disagree

2. The slide presentation reinforced the lecture material.

   1 Strongly agree
   2 Agree
   3 Neutral/Undecided
   4 Disagree
   5 Strongly disagree

3. The overhead transparencies used by the librarian helped to make the presentation more organized and easier to follow.

   1 Strongly agree
   2 Agree
   3 Neutral/Undecided
   4 Disagree
   5 Strongly disagree

4. The transparencies were easy to see on the projection screen.

   1 Strongly agree
   2 Agree
   3 Neutral/Undecided
   4 Disagree
   5 Strongly disagree

5. The examples on the transparencies were too small to be easily read.

   1 Strongly agree
   2 Agree
   3 Neutral/Undecided
   4 Disagree
   5 Strongly disagree

6. What might we do to improve the slide presentation?

III. Videotapes

1. The objective of this video, <state objective here>, was clear.

    1   Strongly agree

    2   Agree

    3   Neutral/Undecided

    4   Disagree

    5   Strongly disagree

2. The portion of the video on <blank> was instructive.

    1   Strongly agree

    2   Agree

    3   Neutral/Undecided

    4   Disagree

    5   Strongly disagree

3. The portion of the video on <blank> was <u>too</u> long.

    1   Strongly agree

    2   Agree

    3   Neutral/Undecided

    4   Disagree

    5   Strongly disagree

4. This video made me more aware of the how the <Blank> Library is <e.g., linked to the rest of the campus>.

    1   Strongly agree

    2   Agree

    3   Neutral/Undecided

    4   Disagree

    5   Strongly disagree

5. The video made me more aware of how technological changes have affected libraries.

    1   Strongly agree

    2   Agree

    3   Neutral/Undecided

    4   Disagree

    5   Strongly disagree

6. The information in the video was presented <u>too</u> quickly.

    1   Strongly agree

    2   Agree

    3   Neutral/Undecided

    4   Disagree

    5   Strongly disagree

7. The video was <u>too</u> long.

    1   Strongly agree

    2   Agree

    3   Neutral/Undecided

    4   Disagree

    5   Strongly disagree

8. The audio portion in the video was easy to understand.

    1   Strongly agree

    2   Agree

    3   Neutral/Undecided

    4   Disagree

    5   Strongly disagree

9. The video portion of the tape illustrated the main ideas of the script.

    1   Strongly agree

    2   Agree

    3   Neutral/Undecided

    4   Disagree

    5   Strongly disagree

10. Watching this video increased my interest in learning about the Library.

    1   Strongly agree
    2   Agree
    3   Neutral/Undecided
    4   Disagree
    5   Strongly disagree

11. Viewing videos helped to make search strategies more understandable.

    1   Strongly agree
    2   Agree
    3   Neutral/Undecided
    4   Disagree
    5   Strongly disagree

12. Viewing a video helped to explain <e.g., name of library resource>.

    1   Strongly agree
    2   Agree
    3   Neutral/Undecided
    4   Disagree
    5   Strongly disagree

13. I enjoyed watching this video.

    1   Strongly agree
    2   Agree
    3   Neutral/Undecided
    4   Disagree
    5   Strongly disagree

14. The videotape provided a good explanation of the library research process.

    1   Strongly agree
    2   Agree
    3   Neutral/Undecided
    4   Disagree
    5   Strongly disagree

15. Do you have any comments on how the video could be improved?

IV. Demonstrations of Electronic Resources

1. Seeing the online catalog demonstrated was <u>not</u> a useful way to learn how to use it.

    1   Strongly agree
    2   Agree
    3   Neutral/Undecided
    4   Disagree
    5   Strongly disagree

2. The on-screen projection of the online catalog was clear and easy to read.

    1   Strongly agree
    2   Agree
    3   Neutral/Undecided
    4   Disagree
    5   Strongly disagree

3. The lab period will help me to use the online catalog effectively.

    1   Strongly agree
    2   Agree
    3   Neutral/Undecided
    4   Disagree
    5   Strongly disagree

4. Seeing the CD-ROM indexes demonstrated was a useful way to learn how to use periodical indexes.

    1   Strongly agree
    2   Agree
    3   Neutral/Undecided
    4   Disagree
    5   Strongly disagree

5. The CD-ROM lab period was helpful for understanding computer indexes.

    1   Strongly agree

    2   Agree

    3   Neutral/Undecided

    4   Disagree

    5   Strongly disagree

6. The examples in the online demonstration were <u>not</u> relevant to my research assignment.

    1   Strongly agree

    2   Agree

    3   Neutral/Undecided

    4   Disagree

    5   Strongly disagree

7. Demonstrations of sample GOPHER searches significantly contributed to my understanding of the Internet.

    1   Strongly agree

    2   Agree

    3   Neutral/Undecided

    4   Disagree

    5   Strongly disagree

8. The online catalog <or CD-ROM or Internet> demonstration was:

    ____ too long

    ____ just right

    ____ too short

9. How do you think our instruction of the online catalog could be improved?

10. If you could use <Lexis/Nexis/DIALOG><blank> as often as you wanted, how often would that be?

    ____ More than once a week

    ____ Once a week

    ____ Once or twice a month

    ____ Once or twice a semester

    ____ Hardly ever

11. Are there any search features on the system that you find particularly difficult to understand or use effectively? Please describe:

12. Do you feel that you need further instruction in using <<blank> CD-ROM/the online catalog/<blank> database>?

___ Yes

___ No

V. Computer-Aided Instruction (CAI)

1. The computer tutorials taught me how to use the <Blank> CD-ROM database.

    1   Strongly agree
    2   Agree
    3   Neutral/Undecided
    4   Disagree
    5   Strongly disagree

2. The online "help" made the <Blank> CD-ROM easier to understand.

    1   Strongly agree
    2   Agree
    3   Neutral/Undecided
    4   Disagree
    5   Strongly disagree

3. The computer tutorial taught me the basics of using the online catalog.

    1   Strongly agree
    2   Agree
    3   Neutral/Undecided
    4   Disagree
    5   Strongly disagree

4. I prefer using computer tutorials to having a demonstration for learning to use <blank>.

    1   Strongly agree

    2   Agree

    3   Neutral/Undecided

    4   Disagree

    5   Strongly disagree

5. Use the scale below to indicate your degree of agreement with the statements about the computer lab/workshop you attended. Fill in your answers with a pencil on the attached computer answer sheet.

    1   Strongly agree

    2   Agree

    3   Neutral/Undecided

    4   Disagree

    5   Strongly disagree

Electronic formats:

    a)   The computer equipment used for this class was excellent.

    b)   The equipment was in good working order.

    c)   The computers were <u>not</u> available for use when I needed them for my assignment/project.

    d)   I had trouble scheduling time with the computer/CD-ROM.

    e)   I had no problems using the <blank> CD-ROM that my instructor required me to use for my assignment.

    f)   The CD-ROMs available in the <Blank> Library met my academic needs.

    g)   The handouts on Veronica/Archie/FTP, etc. were clear and easy to understand.

    h)   The demonstration of Netscape/Mosaic increased my understanding of the Internet.

    i)   The hands-on time made understanding the <blank> database easier.

    j)   The instructor had a good working knowledge of the computer equipment.

    k)   The instructor explained the databases/online services completely.

    l)   The instructor's teaching ability and overall knowledge of the computer software enabled me to learn the software easily.

    m)   The instructor did a good job of making the computer database easy to use.

    n)   The instructor did a good job of explaining the use of the Internet.

SECTION 7
Evaluation of Specific Resources

Evaluating the resource tools presented in an instruction session provides the librarian with valuable information that can be analyzed to determine whether users benefited from the instruction and to improve future sessions. This section deals with evaluating specialized resource tools. The resulting data provide feedback on the strengths and weaknesses of certain tools, documentation that certain resources are more valuable than others, and ideas for improving or modifying the instruction.

This section of questions has been prepared so that any item or specific tool within a list may be added or deleted, depending on the individual library setting. Instructors should select *only* those resources found in their library and pertinent to their specific program. For instance, a general orientation session for elementary children, in a school or public library, may not include instruction in use of the Internet, but will explain the catalog or sample periodical citations from the *Readers' Guide to Periodical Literature*. On the other hand, library orientation for a college course on cell biology will require detailed instruction of various CD-ROMs, online searching, and the Internet. Most of the questions in this section are designed to ask about a mix of special resources used in instruction rather than a single element or tool.

Suggested Readings

Adams, Mignon M. "Evaluation." In *Sourcebook for Bibliographic Instruction*. Chicago: American Library Association, 1993.

Adams, Mignon M., Mary Loe, T. Mark Morey, and Robert E. Schell. *Evaluating a Library Instruction Program: A Case Study of Effective Intracampus Cooperation*. Oswego, N.Y.: State University of New York College at Oswego, <1983>. ERIC ED 274378.

Association of College and Research Libraries. Bibliographic Instruction Section. Subcommittee on Evaluation. *Evaluating Bibliographic Instruction*. Chicago: American Library Association, 1983.

OUTLINE OF SECTION 7

Evaluation of Specific Resources

   I.   Instructor's Evaluation

  II.   Student Knowledge

 III.   Resource Methods

  IV.   Tools

   V.   Specific Aspects of the Instruction

I. Instructor's Evaluation

1. Please indicate the importance of the following tools to your students. Use a scale of 1 to 5, with 1 being the highest positive score.

	High				Low
<Catalog>	1	2	3	4	5
Internet	1	2	3	4	5
Periodical indexes and abstracts	1	2	3	4	5
CD-ROM indexes/Databases	1	2	3	4	5
Online Searching (DIALOG, BRS, Other)	1	2	3	4	5
Encyclopedias, almanacs, handbooks	1	2	3	4	5
Bibliographies	1	2	3	4	5
Humanities sources	1	2	3	4	5
Social sciences sources	1	2	3	4	5
Science sources	1	2	3	4	5

II. Student Knowledge

1. Identify the following parts of a sample periodical citation from the *Readers' Guide to Periodical Literature:*

    Baker, Ruth Ann. "Children's lit-crit (sarcastic criticism of role models in children's literature)." *National Review,* 46(2): 56 (Feb. 7, 1994).

    Author: _____

    Journal: _____

    Volume: _____

    Date: _____

2. Identify the following items from a sample book citation in the catalog.

    Dickens, Charles. *Oliver Twist.* London: Oxford University Press, 1981. (PR 4567 A1 1981)

    Author: _____

    Title: _____

    Publisher: _____

    Date: _____

    Call # _____

3. This session has given me adequate understanding of and skill in using: (*Circle one number for each item.*)

        a) the online catalog.

                1   Strongly agree

                2   Agree

                3   Neutral/Undecided

                4   Disagree

                5   Strongly disagree

        b) the Internet.

                1   Strongly agree

                2   Agree

                3   Neutral/Undecided

                4   Disagree

                5   Strongly disagree

        c) *Library of Congress Subject Headings.*

                1   Strongly agree

                2   Agree

                3   Neutral/Undecided

                4   Disagree

                5   Strongly disagree

        d) the various periodical indexes and abstracts.

                1   Strongly agree

                2   Agree

                3   Neutral/Undecided

                4   Disagree

                5   Strongly disagree

4. What library use was needed to complete the requirements of this course?

        ____ Reserve readings

        ____ Online catalog

        ____ Index & abstract volumes to locate periodical articles

        ____ CD-ROM databases

        ____ Other (please specify)

III. Resource Methods

1. Length of presentation relating to each of the following was: *(Check one column for each item.)*

	Too long	About right	Too short
Information/Reference services	_____	_____	_____
Circulation services/Privileges	_____	_____	_____
Library tour	_____	_____	_____
Photocopying/Document delivery	_____	_____	_____
Interlibrary loan	_____	_____	_____
Reserve	_____	_____	_____

2. Based on this library experience, would you like the library instruction to spend more, less, or the same amount of time on the following topics? *(Circle one answer for each item on the list.)*

Card/online catalog	More	Same	Less
Search strategy	More	Same	Less
Finding books	More	Same	Less
Using the Internet	More	Same	Less
Using periodical indexes	More	Same	Less
Using CD-ROM products	More	Same	Less
Finding periodicals	More	Same	Less
Finding newspaper indexes	More	Same	Less
Finding and using microforms	More	Same	Less
Explaining library privileges	More	Same	Less
Other topics (please specify)	More	Same	Less
_____	More	Same	Less
_____	More	Same	Less

Evaluation of Specific Resources | 59

IV. Tools

1. Which of the items we discussed did you find most useful?   (*Please number in order of most importance to you: 1 = highest; 10 = lowest.*)

Note: This list may vary depending on your needs.

General library information   _____

Subject headings   _____

Catalog   _____

Reference sources (e.g., encyclopedias, bibliographies, etc.)   _____

Indexes (e.g., *Readers' Guide to Periodical Literature*)   _____

CD-ROM products   _____

Computer searching   _____

Interlibrary loan   _____

The Internet   _____

Other (Please specify)   _____

2. Please evaluate each of the following aspects of the <e.g., class/workshop>.

	Extremely helpful				Not at all helpful
Overview of library (and tour)	1	2	3	4	5
Catalog explanation	1	2	3	4	5
List of subject headings	1	2	3	4	5
Online demonstration	1	2	3	4	5
Reference sources	1	2	3	4	5
Video	1	2	3	4	5
Periodical indexes & abstracts	1	2	3	4	5
The Internet	1	2	3	4	5
Computer searching	1	2	3	4	5
Interlibrary loan	1	2	3	4	5
Handouts	1	2	3	4	5
Instructor	1	2	3	4	5
Other (Please specify)	1	2	3	4	5

3. The information covered, on each of the topics below, was new to me. (*Circle one number for each phase to indicate your agreement with this statement.*)

	Definitely yes				Definitely no
Phase I: Finding books in the catalog	1	2	3	4	5
Phase II: Using periodical indexes	1	2	3	4	5
Phase III: Doing an annotated bibliography	1	2	3	4	5

V. Specific Aspects of the Instruction

1. Of the material presented, I knew: (*Check one.*)

___ all of it
___ most of it
___ some of it
___ little of it
___ none of it

2. Did you become aware of potential information sources with which you were not previously familiar?

    ___ Yes

    ___ No

    ___ Don't know

3. Please list the aspects of this session that were valuable to you.

4. What part of the library lecture/exercise did you find the *most* useful? (*Number the top three from 1 to 3, with 1 being the top.*)

    ___ general information about <Blank> Library

    ___ specific information about <Blank> Learning Resources Center

    ___ specific information about <Blank> Undergraduate Library

    ___ how to use the <card catalog/online catalog>

    ___ how to use the *Readers' Guide to Periodical Literature*

    ___ how to use the <Blank> CD-ROM database

    ___ Other; please describe _____

5. What part of the lecture/exercise did you find least useful? (*Number the top three from 1 to 3, with 1 being the least useful.*)

    ___ general information about <Blank> Library

    ___ specific information about <Blank> Learning Resources Center

    ___ specific information about <Blank> Undergraduate Library

    ___ how to use the <card catalog/online catalog>

    ___ how to use the *Readers' Guide to Periodical Literature*

    ___ how to use the <Blank> CD-ROM database

    ___ everything was useful to me

    ___ other; please list below:

6. In what areas would you have preferred more instruction?

SECTION 8
Assignments and Other Course Activities

Many instruction sessions include integral assignments or activities. Such assignments should flow naturally from the instruction and be individualized to meet students' needs. There is a relationship between these activities and academic achievement: learning and practicing what is taught is essential to mastering materials and information resources. When you devise and evaluate assignments, whether in a school or academic library setting, consider the following questions:

> Do the length and complexity of the assignment match the determined need?
>
> Is the assignment relevant to the instruction or just "busy work"?
>
> Is the assignment interesting enough to bring about student learning or is it just frustrating?
>
> Can the assignment be graded or effectively evaluated?

Assignments that include hands-on interaction with library tools or resources, whether print or electronic, are most likely to promote measurable learning. Individualizing the assignments will encourage students to do their own work and save wear and tear on the resources.

Testing is one method of evaluating learning, but tests must be relevant to the information taught and the learning objectives of the session or class. If assignments and exams are to be graded the grading policies must be clear from the outset. *Don't* assign anything you don't want to grade.

Suggested Readings

Roberts, Anne F., and Susan G. Blandy. *Library Instruction for Librarians.* 2nd rev. ed. Englewood, Colo.: Libraries Unlimited, 1989.

Turner, Philip M. "Evaluation." In *Helping Teachers Teach: A School Library Media Specialist's Role.* 2nd ed. Englewood, Colo.: Libraries Unlimited, 1993.

OUTLINE OF SECTION 8

Assignments and Other Course Activities

I. Assignments

II. Evaluating Exams and Tests

III. Grading Policy

IV. Evaluating the Evaluation Form

I. Assignments

Please evaluate the assignments in this session with regard to the following statements. (*Circle the number that corresponds to your opinion.*)

1. The assignments were well planned.

1 Strongly agree
2 Agree
3 Neutral/Undecided
4 Disagree
5 Strongly disagree

2. The assignment instructions were clear.

1 Strongly agree
2 Agree
3 Neutral/Undecided
4 Disagree
5 Strongly disagree

3. The assignments correlated with the lectures.

1 Strongly agree
2 Agree
3 Neutral/Undecided
4 Disagree
5 Strongly disagree

4. The content of the presentation was clearly related to the class assignment(s).

1 Strongly agree
2 Agree
3 Neutral/Undecided
4 Disagree
5 Strongly disagree

5. The assignments were relevant to my course work.

    1   Strongly agree
    2   Agree
    3   Neutral/Undecided
    4   Disagree
    5   Strongly disagree

6. This presentation will help me with my <blank> assignment.

    1   Strongly agree
    2   Agree
    3   Neutral/Undecided
    4   Disagree
    5   Strongly disagree

7. Overall, the information presented was (or will be) useful to me in the course of completing my library assignment(s).

    1   Strongly agree
    2   Agree
    3   Neutral/Undecided
    4   Disagree
    5   Strongly disagree

8. The assignments in this session (term project, self-guided tour, etc.) contributed significantly to my understanding of the library and research process.

    1   Strongly agree
    2   Agree
    3   Neutral/Undecided
    4   Disagree
    5   Strongly disagree

9. The assignment's directions were clear—that is, you understood what was expected of you and when the assignments were due.

    1   Strongly agree
    2   Agree
    3   Neutral/Undecided
    4   Disagree
    5   Strongly disagree

If unclear, how could they be improved?

10. The assigned reading was appropriate.

      1   Strongly agree

      2   Agree

      3   Neutral/Undecided

      4   Disagree

      5   Strongly disagree

11. The term project provided an opportunity to apply what was learned in this session.

      1   Strongly agree

      2   Agree

      3   Neutral/Undecided

      4   Disagree

      5   Strongly disagree

12. The <blank> exercise was helpful.

      1   Strongly agree

      2   Agree

      3   Neutral/Undecided

      4   Disagree

      5   Strongly disagree

13. This session made it easier for me to use the library for assignments for this and/or other courses.

      1   Strongly agree

      2   Agree

      3   Neutral/Undecided

      4   Disagree

      5   Strongly disagree

14. Did you use the information from the library presentation for a class assignment this semester?

      Yes ___   No ___

15. Please rate the following: (*Circle the number of your response.*)

Assignments were:

    1   Excellent

    2   Good

    3   Satisfactory

    4   Fair

    5   Poor

The term project was:

    1   Excellent

    2   Good

    3   Satisfactory

    4   Fair

    5   Poor

16. Overall I would rate the quality of the weekly assignments as: (*Check one.*)

___ Excellent   ___ Good   ___ Satisfactory   ___ Fair   ___ Poor

17. The library exercise was: (Check one.)

___ too long

___ about right

___ too short

18. How effective were each of the following in achieving the course's goals and objectives? (*Check one space in each row.*)

	Very effective	Somewhat effective	Neutral	Somewhat ineffective	Very ineffective	Not applicable
Labs	_____	_____	_____	_____	_____	_____
Papers	_____	_____	_____	_____	_____	_____
Problem sets	_____	_____	_____	_____	_____	_____

II. Evaluating Exams and Tests

1. The midterm was:

___ too easy

___ about right

___ too difficult

2. Assignments and exams reflected the subject matter.

1   Strongly agree

2   Agree

3   Neutral/Undecided

4   Disagree

5   Strongly disagree

3. Examinations were:

1   Excellent

2   Good

3   Satisfactory

4   Fair

5   Poor

4. The tests were relevant to the course content.

1   Strongly agree

2   Agree

3   Neutral/Undecided

4   Disagree

5   Strongly disagree

5. The examinations covered the materials presented in class.

1   Strongly agree

2   Agree

3   Neutral/Undecided

4   Disagree

5   Strongly disagree

6. The final exam was fair and appropriate to the course material.

   1   Strongly agree
   2   Agree
   3   Neutral/Undecided
   4   Disagree
   5   Strongly disagree

7. The number of tests enabled me to evaluate my progress.

   1   Strongly agree
   2   Agree
   3   Neutral/Undecided
   4   Disagree
   5   Strongly disagree

8. Please indicate your degree of agreement with the following statements on the attached answer sheet, using the categories listed below.

   1   Strongly agree
   2   Agree
   3   Neutral/Undecided
   4   Disagree
   5   Strongly disagree

   a)   Tests reflected lectures, handouts, and assigned materials.

   b)   Tests included vague or tricky items.

   c)   The test format was simple and direct.

   d)   Tests/Assignments were returned promptly.

   e)   The exam was too long.

   f)   The instructor was fair in evaluation practices.

   g)   The material on the tests had been presented thoroughly in class.

   h)   The material on tests covered the most important points in the session.

III. Grading Policy

1. The requirements for the course and grading system were distributed and explained the first week of class.

    1   Strongly agree
    2   Agree
    3   Neutral/Undecided
    4   Disagree
    5   Strongly disagree

2. The course requirements and grading system were clear from the start.

    1   Strongly agree
    2   Agree
    3   Neutral/Undecided
    4   Disagree
    5   Strongly disagree

3. The grading was fair.

    1   Strongly agree
    2   Agree
    3   Neutral/Undecided
    4   Disagree
    5   Strongly disagree

IV. Evaluating the Evaluation Form

1. This form allowed me adequately to evaluate the library presentation.

        1   Strongly agree

        2   Agree

        3   Neutral/Undecided

        4   Disagree

        5   Strongly disagree

2. This form allowed me adequately to evaluate the instructor.

        1   Strongly agree

        2   Agree

        3   Neutral/Undecided

        4   Disagree

        5   Strongly disagree

SECTION 9
Special Instruction Methods

Librarians use various special instruction methods to orient students to the library and assist them with their research and information needs. Many of these methods involve one-time interaction rather than a series of sessions. This type of instruction includes library tours, assistance at the reference desk, term paper consultations, and high school visits to academic libraries. Other special methods, such as field trips and author visits, may occur only once *within* a program that meets several times. Because so many of these special methods are one-time events, librarians often neglect to evaluate their effectiveness.

They should, instead, plan ways to evaluate them ahead of time. Whether contact is made at the reference desk or during a prearranged appointment or session, librarians must determine if it achieved the intended results. For example, patrons usually take only one orientation tour. However it is presented (e.g., audiotaped, videotaped, self-guided, or led by library staff), it should achieve some purpose. Librarians need to know if it reached the intended audience and if it included information to enable that audience to use the library more efficiently and effectively. Reference desk assistance

and term paper consultations also provide unique opportunities for individualized instruction and evaluation.

Even classes or programs in library instruction have special aspects such as reserve readings or case studies that can evaluated separately. Evaluation of all of these special instruction methods requires planning and forethought. The sample questions in this section can be asked at the end of the instruction or at various points in an extended course or workshop.

Suggested Readings

Rice, James. "Strategies for Library Instruction." In *Teaching Library Use: A Guide for Library Instruction.* Westport, Conn.: Greenwood Press, 1981.

Roberts, Anne F., and Susan G. Blandy. "Choosing Formats." In *Library Instruction for Librarians.* Englewood, Colo.: Libraries Unlimited, 1989.

Simons, Michael. "Evaluation of Library Tours." Reno: Nevada University, Reno, 1990. ERIC ED 331513.

OUTLINE OF SECTION 9

Special Instruction Methods

I.   Tours

II. Reference Librarian or Point-of-Use Instruction

III. Consultation or Term Paper Assistance

IV. General Course Materials and Activities

V.   Special Presentation Methods

I. Tours

1. The tour leader spoke loudly enough for everyone to hear.

    1   Strongly agree
    2   Agree
    3   Neutral/Undecided
    4   Disagree
    5   Strongly disagree

2. The tour group was just the right size.

    1   Strongly agree
    2   Agree
    3   Neutral/Undecided
    4   Disagree
    5   Strongly disagree

3. The tour group was too large.

    1   Strongly agree
    2   Agree
    3   Neutral/Undecided
    4   Disagree
    5   Strongly disagree

4. The tour leader was knowledgeable about <blank>.

    1   Strongly agree
    2   Agree
    3   Neutral/Undecided
    4   Disagree
    5   Strongly disagree

5. The tour of the Library helped me to understand the location of specific library services, collections, and facilities.

    1   Strongly agree
    2   Agree
    3   Neutral/Undecided
    4   Disagree
    5   Strongly disagree

6. The self-guided tour helped me learn about the basic services, collection, and facilities of <Blank> Library.

      1   Strongly agree

      2   Agree

      3   Neutral/Undecided

      4   Disagree

      5   Strongly disagree

7. I prefer the self-guided tour to a tour led by library staff.

      1   Strongly agree

      2   Agree

      3   Neutral/Undecided

      4   Disagree

      5   Strongly disagree

II. Reference Librarian or Point-of-Use Instruction

1. The reference librarians were helpful in doing the assignments.

      1   Strongly agree

      2   Agree

      3   Neutral/Undecided

      4   Disagree

      5   Strongly disagree

2. A librarian at the Reference Desk was helpful in constructing a search strategy.

      1   Strongly agree

      2   Agree

      3   Neutral/Undecided

      4   Disagree

      5   Strongly disagree

3. The librarian at the Reference Desk was helpful.

    1   Strongly agree

    2   Agree

    3   Neutral/Undecided

    4   Disagree

    5   Strongly disagree

4. The school media specialist was helpful in locating material for my paper.

    1   Strongly agree

    2   Agree

    3   Neutral/Undecided

    4   Disagree

    5   Strongly disagree

III. Consultation or Term Paper Assistance

1. The librarian understood my research project.

    1   Strongly agree

    2   Agree

    3   Neutral/Undecided

    4   Disagree

    5   Strongly disagree

2. I felt free to ask questions or comment during the consultation.

    1   Strongly agree

    2   Agree

    3   Neutral/Undecided

    4   Disagree

    5   Strongly disagree

3. The opportunity to talk to other participants was valuable.

    1   Strongly agree

    2   Agree

    3   Neutral/Undecided

    4   Disagree

    5   Strongly disagree

4. My consultation with the librarian was helpful.

    1   Strongly agree

    2   Agree

    3   Neutral/Undecided

    4   Disagree

    5   Strongly disagree

5. The term paper consultation appointment was helpful.

    1   Strongly agree

    2   Agree

    3   Neutral/Undecided

    4   Disagree

    5   Strongly disagree

6. Was consultation about a research project in your major field?

    Yes ___ No ___

    If no, please specify which field _____

7. What was the reason for the consultation?

    ___ Research/Seminar paper

    ___ Master's thesis

    ___ Ph.D. dissertation

    ___ Book/Article

    ___ Other (personal interest, etc.)

8. Were you aware that you could arrange for consultations with a reference librarian before this program was advertised?

    ___ Yes

    ___ No

9. Had you ever discussed research or library problems with a reference librarian before this consultation?

    ___ Never discussed

    ___ 1 to 3 times

    ___ 4 to 6 times

    ___ More than 6 times

10. Did the consultation provide the kind of assistance you expected?   (*Check one.*)

    very helpful ___   somewhat helpful ___   of little help ___

    Additional comments:

11. Did you discuss the library exercise with a librarian?

    ___ Yes

    ___ No

IV. General Course Materials and Activities

Please rate the quality of the following elements of the library <session/class/presentation> relative to your assignments: (*Circle the number on the scale that most nearly describes your feelings.*)

1. Reserve readings

    1 ——— 2 ——— 3 ——— 4 ——— 5
    Excellent   Poor

2. Case studies

    1 ——— 2 ——— 3 ——— 4 ——— 5
    Excellent   Poor

3. Bulletin board

    1 ———— 2 ———— 3 ———— 4 ———— 5
    Excellent   Poor

4. Annotated bibliography

    1 ———— 2 ———— 3 ———— 4 ———— 5
    Excellent   Poor

5. Research proposal

    1 ———— 2 ———— 3 ———— 4 ———— 5
    Excellent   Poor

6. Peer review of proposals and drafts

    1 ———— 2 ———— 3 ———— 4 ———— 5
    Excellent   Poor

7. Class discussion

    1 ———— 2 ———— 3 ———— 4 ———— 5
    Excellent   Poor

8. Videos

    1 ———— 2 ———— 3 ———— 4 ———— 5
    Excellent   Poor

9. Research paper

    1 ———— 2 ———— 3 ———— 4 ———— 5
    Excellent   Poor

10. Library materials

    1 ———— 2 ———— 3 ———— 4 ———— 5
    Excellent   Poor

11. Searching techniques

$$1 \underline{\qquad} 2 \underline{\qquad} 3 \underline{\qquad} 4 \underline{\qquad} 5$$
Excellent   Poor

V. Special Presentation Methods

1. Guest speakers during the course helped to make the subject matter more understandable.

  1 Strongly agree
  2 Agree
  3 Neutral/Undecided
  4 Disagree
  5 Strongly disagree

2. Reviewing case studies helped to make the subject matter more understandable.

  1 Strongly agree
  2 Agree
  3 Neutral/Undecided
  4 Disagree
  5 Strongly disagree

3. Field trips helped to make subject matter more understandable.

  1 Strongly agree
  2 Agree
  3 Neutral/Undecided
  4 Disagree
  5 Strongly disagree

4. The author visit provided my students with greater insight into the writing process.

  1 Strongly agree
  2 Agree
  3 Neutral/Undecided
  4 Disagree
  5 Strongly disagree

5. Listening to lectures about the library's collections, services, and facilities helped to make them more understandable.

    1   Strongly agree

    2   Agree

    3   Neutral/Undecided

    4   Disagree

    5   Strongly disagree

6. Listening and watching the instructor describe, explain, and show reference books made their use more understandable.

    1   Strongly agree

    2   Agree

    3   Neutral/Undecided

    4   Disagree

    5   Strongly disagree

7. Participating in discussions helped to make library resources and search strategies more understandable.

    1   Strongly agree

    2   Agree

    3   Neutral/Undecided

    4   Disagree

    5   Strongly disagree

8. Writing exercises and assignments helped to make library resources and search strategies more understandable.

    1   Strongly agree

    2   Agree

    3   Neutral/Undecided

    4   Disagree

    5   Strongly disagree

9. Small group activities helped to make library resources and search strategies more understandable.

    1   Strongly agree

    2   Agree

    3   Neutral/Undecided

    4   Disagree

    5   Strongly disagree

10. Below is a selected list of library instruction methods. Using the following scale from 1 through 5, please indicate which ones you would prefer to use in learning about the library.

    1   Very desirable

    2   Somewhat desirable

    3   Neutral/Undecided

    4   Somewhat undesirable

    5   Very undesirable

____ a) Orientation by librarian for entire class at one time.

____ b) Asking at the Reference Desk only when in need of assistance.

____ c) Meeting with a librarian person-to-person when a library research project has been assigned.

SECTION 10
Interaction with the Teacher

The interaction between the librarian and the classroom teacher or academic faculty member is critical to determining the effectiveness of library instruction in meeting students' needs. Librarian-teacher teamwork may be directly related to student learning. If this teamwork is to be encouraged and expanded, care must be taken in planning the students' library experience and the results must be evaluated and used for future planning. Both the librarian and the teacher must understand the goals and objectives of the library experience and agree on the expected outcome of the instruction. An especially notable example of teamwork involves the school librarian or media specialist, who often actively helps the teacher to teach.

Suggested Readings

Jacobson, Gertrude N., and Michael J. Albright. "Motivation Via Videotape: Key to Undergraduate Library Instruction in the Research Library." *Journal of Academic Librarianship* 9 (November 1983): 270–75.

Puryear, Dorothy. "Computer-Aided Instruction for Literacy in Libraries." *Catholic Library World* 64 (October–March 1993–94): 40–42.

Simmons-O'Neill, Elizabeth. "Evaluating Sources: Strategies for Faculty-Librarian-Student Collaboration." March 1990. ERIC ED 321259.

Turner, Philip M. *Helping Teachers to Teach: A School Library Media Specialist's Role.* 2nd ed. Englewood, Colo.: Libraries Unlimited, 1993.

OUTLINE OF SECTION 10

Interaction with the Teacher

I. Interaction with the Classroom Teacher/Instructor

II. Appropriateness of the Instruction

I. Interaction with the Classroom Teacher/Instructor

1. I feel comfortable contacting the <blank (e.g., Coordinator of Library Instruction)> to arrange library presentations for my class(es).

    1   Strongly agree
    2   Agree
    3   Neutral/Undecided
    4   Disagree
    5   Strongly disagree

2. I will continue to schedule library presentations for my class(es).

    1   Strongly agree
    2   Agree
    3   Neutral/Undecided
    4   Disagree
    5   Strongly disagree

3. Team planning of units between librarians and classroom teachers has been helpful.

    1   Strongly agree
    2   Agree
    3   Neutral/Undecided
    4   Disagree
    5   Strongly disagree

4. Lessons planned cooperatively by librarians and classroom teachers provided satisfactory levels of resources.

    1   Strongly agree
    2   Agree
    3   Neutral/Undecided
    4   Disagree
    5   Strongly disagree

5. The name of the subject librarian who has liaison responsibilities with my department is _____ .

II. Appropriateness of the Instruction

1. The librarian's presentation inspired interest in <blank> on the part of my students.

      1   Strongly agree

      2   Agree

      3   Neutral/Undecided

      4   Disagree

      5   Strongly disagree

2. The librarian stimulated good student discussion during the library presentation.

      1   Strongly agree

      2   Agree

      3   Neutral/Undecided

      4   Disagree

      5   Strongly disagree

3. The content level of the library presentation was appropriate to the grade level of my assignment.

      1   Strongly agree

      2   Agree

      3   Neutral/Undecided

      4   Disagree

      5   Strongly disagree

4. The library presentation instruction level was appropriate to the grade level of my class.

      1   Strongly agree

      2   Agree

      3   Neutral/Undecided

      4   Disagree

      5   Strongly disagree

5. The overall quality of the library presentation given to my class(es) was excellent.

    1   Strongly agree

    2   Agree

    3   Neutral/Undecided

    4   Disagree

    5   Strongly disagree

6. The teaching format of this library presentation addressed the needs of my students.

    1   Strongly agree

    2   Agree

    3   Neutral/Undecided

    4   Disagree

    5   Strongly disagree

7. The information provided at the library presentation was at the right level for my students.

    1   Strongly agree

    2   Agree

    3   Neutral/Undecided

    4   Disagree

    5   Strongly disagree

8. My students left the library presentation with an understanding of basic services, collections, and facilities.

    1   Strongly agree

    2   Agree

    3   Neutral/Undecided

    4   Disagree

    5   Strongly disagree

9. The resource examples were appropriate for the needs of my class.

    1   Strongly agree

    2   Agree

    3   Neutral/Undecided

    4   Disagree

    5   Strongly disagree

10. The library presentation related to my course objectives as stated by me during my initial meeting with the librarian.

       1   Strongly agree
       2   Agree
       3   Neutral/Undecided
       4   Disagree
       5   Strongly disagree

11. Essential points were missing from the library presentation.

       1   Strongly agree
       2   Agree
       3   Neutral/Undecided
       4   Disagree
       5   Strongly disagree

12. The presentation was appropriate to students in terms of their level of education and research experience.

       1   Strongly agree
       2   Agree
       3   Neutral/Undecided
       4   Disagree
       5   Strongly disagree

13. Correlation of the content to the students' knowledge level was:

___ Superior   ___ Very Good   ___ Good   ___ Fair   ___ Poor

14. Was the level of instruction appropriate for your class(es)?

___ Yes   ___ For most students   ___ No

If "No," was it   ___ too elementary   ___ too complex

___ other? _____

15. The presentations include the information needed by my students to complete their library-related assignment.

___ Yes   ___ No   ___ Don't know

16. Given our mutual objectives, appropriate information was given to enable students to locate and use: (*Check all that apply.*)

    ___ the general, circulating collection
    ___ the layout of the library
    ___ the card catalog
    ___ subject headings
    ___ the reference collection
    ___ periodical indexes
    ___ periodicals
        ___ current issues
        ___ back loose issues
        ___ microfilm
    ___ reserve materials
    ___ nonprint materials
    ___ nonprint equipment
    ___ other

SECTION 11
Presentation and Content

Questions in this section solicit patrons' attitudes and opinions regarding the presentation and content of library instruction. For presentations ranging from orientation tours to multiple-session BI courses, the questions explore elements such as organization, timing, and the relevance, amount, and difficulty of the material covered (but not the role of the library instructor, the subject of Section 12).

As presentation-giving is essentially teaching, when librarians lead a tour, class, or workshop they want and expect the participants to learn something. Yet they seldom undertake detailed testing of content retention as a means of evaluating the presentation's effectiveness. In this section, general questions on presentation and content are followed by questions on the relevance and success of specific types of presentations (e.g., workshops, lectures, or demonstrations of a specific tool).

Suggested Reading

Roberts, Anne F., and Susan G. Blandy. *Library Instruction for Librarians.* 2nd rev. ed. Englewood, Colo.: Libraries Unlimited, 1989.

OUTLINE OF SECTION 11

Presentation and Content

I. Procedures and Content
- A. General Procedures
- B. Content: Goals and Objectives
- C. Level of Material
- D. Timing/Pace
- E. Length of Presentation
- F. Amount of Material Covered
- G. Organization

II. Single Presentations, Lectures, and Workshops

III. Multiple-Session Library Courses

I. Procedures and Content

A. General Procedures

1. I attended the library \<blank\> held for my \<blank\>.

    1   Yes

    2   No

2. The library \<blank\> started at the scheduled time.

    1   Yes

    2   No

    3   Don't remember

3. The library \<blank\> ended at the scheduled time.

    1   Yes

    2   No

    3   Don't remember

4. There were enough seats and handouts for all participants.

    1   Strongly agree

    2   Agree

    3   Neutral/Undecided

    4   Disagree

    5   Strongly disagree

B. Content: Goals and Objectives

1. The purpose of the library \<blank\> was clear.

    1   Strongly agree

    2   Agree

    3   Neutral/Undecided

    4   Disagree

    5   Strongly disagree

2. The objectives of the library <blank> were clearly stated.

    1   Strongly agree

    2   Agree

    3   Neutral/Undecided

    4   Disagree

    5   Strongly disagree

3. The objectives of the library <blank> were achieved.

    1   Strongly agree

    2   Agree

    3   Neutral/Undecided

    4   Disagree

    5   Strongly disagree

4. The content of the library <blank> I attended was excellent.

    1   Strongly agree

    2   Agree

    3   Neutral/Undecided

    4   Disagree

    5   Strongly disagree

5. <u>Too</u> much information was given at the library <blank>.

    1   Strongly agree

    2   Agree

    3   Neutral/Undecided

    4   Disagree

    5   Strongly disagree

6. Library <blank> examples adequately explained abstract concepts and ideas.

    1   Strongly agree

    2   Agree

    3   Neutral/Undecided

    4   Disagree

    5   Strongly disagree

7. Library <blank> examples were representative of cultural, ethnic, racial, religious, and lifestyle diversity.

    1   Strongly agree

    2   Agree

    3   Neutral/Undecided

    4   Disagree

    5   Strongly disagree

C.   Level of Material

1. The information in the library presentation covered the kinds of sources that I need to complete my specific assignment.

    1   Strongly agree

    2   Agree

    3   Neutral/Undecided

    4   Disagree

    5   Strongly disagree

2. Was the level of instruction: (*Check one.*)

    ___ too elementary?

    ___ about right?

    ___ too difficult?

3. The level of difficulty was: (*Circle one.*)

    1   Very difficult

    2   Somewhat difficult

    3   About right

    4   Somewhat elementary

    5   Very elementary

D. Timing/Pace

1. There was adequate time for the information presented.

   1   Strongly agree
   2   Agree
   3   Neutral/Undecided
   4   Disagree
   5   Strongly disagree

2. The material was presented at an appropriate pace.

   1   Strongly agree
   2   Agree
   3   Neutral/Undecided
   4   Disagree
   5   Strongly disagree

3. Sufficient time was devoted to discussion.

   1   Strongly agree
   2   Agree
   3   Neutral/Undecided
   4   Disagree
   5   Strongly disagree

4. There was enough time to ask questions.

   1   Strongly agree
   2   Agree
   3   Neutral/Undecided
   4   Disagree
   5   Strongly disagree

5. There was enough time for hands-on practice during the library <blank>.

   1   Strongly agree
   2   Agree
   3   Neutral/Undecided
   4   Disagree
   5   Strongly disagree

6. Was the pace of the session:

    ___ too slow?

    ___ about right?

    ___ too fast?

E. Length of Presentation

1. The length of the library presentation was appropriate.

    1   Strongly agree

    2   Agree

    3   Neutral/Undecided

    4   Disagree

    5   Strongly disagree

2. Do you think the library instruction lecture was:

    ___ Too long?

    ___ About the right length?

    ___ Too brief?

Please comment:

3. The length of the presentation was:

    ___ too short

    ___ adequate for expressed needs

    ___ too long

4. The question/review period was:

    ___ too long

    ___ about right

    ___ too short

5. There was <u>not</u> enough opportunity to ask questions.

    1   Strongly agree

    2   Agree

    3   Neutral/Undecided

    4   Disagree

    5   Strongly disagree

6. How would you rate the overall <blank> program in relation to the time spent?

poor	fair	good	very good	excellent
[ ]	[ ]	[ ]	[ ]	[ ]

7. I found the length of the <e.g., training lab> period to be:

too short	adequate	too long
[ ]	[ ]	[ ]

8. The training period was <u>too</u> short.

    1   Strongly agree

    2   Agree

    3   Neutral/Undecided

    4   Disagree

    5   Strongly disagree

F. Amount of Material Covered

1. I was satisfied with the quantity and detail of the library <blank>.

    1   Strongly agree

    2   Agree

    3   Neutral/Undecided

    4   Disagree

    5   Strongly disagree

2. The amount of material presented was appropriate for the time period.

   1   Strongly agree
   2   Agree
   3   Neutral/Undecided
   4   Disagree
   5   Strongly disagree

3. The amount of material presented met the needs of my specific assignment.

   1   Strongly agree
   2   Agree
   3   Neutral/Undecided
   4   Disagree
   5   Strongly disagree

4. The library presentation covered <u>too much</u> material in the time allotted.

   1   Strongly agree
   2   Agree
   3   Neutral/Undecided
   4   Disagree
   5   Strongly disagree

G. Organization

1. The library presentation was <u>not</u> well organized.

   1   Strongly agree
   2   Agree
   3   Neutral/Undecided
   4   Disagree
   5   Strongly disagree

2. During the library presentation, I understood the progression from one topic to the next.

   1   Strongly agree
   2   Agree
   3   Neutral/Undecided
   4   Disagree
   5   Strongly disagree

3. I understood the organization and the subject matter of the library presentation.

    1   Strongly agree

    2   Agree

    3   Neutral/Undecided

    4   Disagree

    5   Strongly disagree

4. I understood the logic and order of the subject matter covered in the library presentation.

    1   Strongly agree

    2   Agree

    3   Neutral/Undecided

    4   Disagree

    5   Strongly disagree

II. Single Presentations, Lectures, and Workshops

1. The library <class/workshop> was an excellent way to learn <e.g., PAIS, SSCI, ERIC>.

    1   Strongly agree

    2   Agree

    3   Neutral/Undecided

    4   Disagree

    5   Strongly disagree

2. The library presentation component of the <e.g., honors colloquium> was excellent.

    1   Strongly agree

    2   Agree

    3   Neutral/Undecided

    4   Disagree

    5   Strongly disagree

3. The library presentation told me about basic services, collections, and facilities in the library that I <u>did not</u> already know about.

    1   Strongly agree

    2   Agree

    3   Neutral/Undecided

    4   Disagree

    5   Strongly disagree

4. When the library presentation covered basic services, collections, and facilities that I <u>already knew</u> <u>about</u>, I found the review helpful.

    1   Strongly agree

    2   Agree

    3   Neutral/Undecided

    4   Disagree

    5   Strongly disagree

5. This presentation will be useful to me in successfully completing my present research assignment.

    1   Strongly agree

    2   Agree

    3   Neutral/Undecided

    4   Disagree

    5   Strongly disagree

6. The library presentation was relevant to my specific need.

    1   Strongly agree

    2   Agree

    3   Neutral/Undecided

    4   Disagree

    5   Strongly disagree

7. Information presented was reinforced by hands-on practice for all participants.

    1   Strongly agree

    2   Agree

    3   Neutral/Undecided

    4   Disagree

    5   Strongly disagree

8. As a result of the presentation, I understand how to use indexes to find periodical articles on my subject.

    1   Strongly agree
    2   Agree
    3   Neutral/Undecided
    4   Disagree
    5   Strongly disagree

9. As a result of the presentation, I understand how to find the issues of periodicals and newspapers owned by the library.

    1   Strongly agree
    2   Agree
    3   Neutral/Undecided
    4   Disagree
    5   Strongly disagree

10. As a result of the library presentation, I understand how to search <Blank> library database(s).

    1   Strongly agree
    2   Agree
    3   Neutral/Undecided
    4   Disagree
    5   Strongly disagree

11. As a result of the library presentation, I understand how to use <blank> reference books.

    1   Strongly agree
    2   Agree
    3   Neutral/Undecided
    4   Disagree
    5   Strongly disagree

12. As a result of the library presentation, I understand how to use a search strategy to organize myself for conducting research.

    1   Strongly agree
    2   Agree
    3   Neutral/Undecided
    4   Disagree
    5   Strongly disagree

III. Multiple-Session Library Courses

1. Course goals and objectives were clearly stated.

   1 Strongly agree
   2 Agree
   3 Neutral/Undecided
   4 Disagree
   5 Strongly disagree

2. I understood the subject matter in this course.

   1 Strongly agree
   2 Agree
   3 Neutral/Undecided
   4 Disagree
   5 Strongly disagree

3. Course materials and expectations were thoroughly outlined and explained.

   1 Strongly agree
   2 Agree
   3 Neutral/Undecided
   4 Disagree
   5 Strongly disagree

4. Course assignments were <u>not</u> clear.

   1 Strongly agree
   2 Agree
   3 Neutral/Undecided
   4 Disagree
   5 Strongly disagree

5. Required readings and texts were valuable.

   1 Strongly agree
   2 Agree
   3 Neutral/Undecided
   4 Disagree
   5 Strongly disagree

6. The course workload relative to other courses at <Blank> for the same number of credits was:

1   Very light
2   Somewhat light
3   About average
4   Somewhat heavy
5   Very heavy

7. The course's workload was evenly distributed throughout the <semester, quarter>.

1   Strongly agree
2   Agree
3   Neutral/Undecided
4   Disagree
5   Strongly disagree

8. The course material was appropriate to the course level.

1   Strongly agree
2   Agree
3   Neutral/Undecided
4   Disagree
5   Strongly disagree

9. The information in this course was useful/relevant.

1   Strongly agree
2   Agree
3   Neutral/Undecided
4   Disagree
5   Strongly disagree

10. The assignments, activities, and tests in <blank> were relevant to the knowledge and skills needed to understand library research and meet the course requirements.

1   Strongly agree
2   Agree
3   Neutral/Undecided
4   Disagree
5   Strongly disagree

11. The class meetings were useful.

    1   Strongly agree

    2   Agree

    3   Neutral/Undecided

    4   Disagree

    5   Strongly disagree

12. In terms of my work for this course, I think the information covered was:

    1   very valuable

    2   valuable

    3   moderately valuable

    4   of little value

    5   of no value

SECTION 12
Evaluating the Instructor

Statements in this section are formulated to solicit the opinions and attitudes of participants about the library presenter or instructor. Evaluation of instructors is difficult to validate, as there is no universal criterion for effective teaching.[1] Often the attitudes about an instruction section are more a reflection of the instructor than of the content or method. Moreover, evaluation of the instructor is especially subjective, in part because of the delicate balance of interaction between individual instructors' and students' personalities. (That is, a specific approach, trait, or mannerism will appeal to some students and not to others.) Nonetheless, instructors must seek to determine whether certain attributes of their manner or presentation style are detrimental to the audience's understanding of the content.

Note that when dealing with highly subjective questions, subtle changes in wording affect responses. Although this section includes many questions, you should select only a small number that are relevant to your program. You should also pretest the questions to ensure that they elicit what you really want to know.

---

1. Marsh, H. W. "Student Evaluation of Teaching," in *The International Encyclopedia of Teaching and Higher Education*, ed. Michael J. Dunkin (Oxford: Pergamon Press, 1987), p. 183.

OUTLINE OF SECTION 12

Evaluating the Instructor

I.   The Librarian or Instructor
    A. Quality of Instructor's Skill
    B. Clarity of Presentation
    C. Preparation and Organization
    D. Teaching Methods
    E. Knowledge of Classroom Assignments
    F. Interactions with Students/Participants
    G. Personal Characteristics and Mannerisms

II. The Teaching Assistant

III. The Instructor of Multiple-Session Library Courses

IV. Quality of the Instructor: Open-Ended Questions

I. The Librarian or Instructor

A. Quality of Instructor's Skill

1. The overall effectiveness of the instructor in the library presentation was excellent.

   1   Strongly agree
   2   Agree
   3   Neutral/Undecided
   4   Disagree
   5   Strongly disagree

2. The instructor's style of presentation held my interest during the <blank>.

   1   Strongly agree
   2   Agree
   3   Neutral/Undecided
   4   Disagree
   5   Strongly disagree

3. The instructor for the library presentation used class time effectively.

   1   Strongly agree
   2   Agree
   3   Neutral/Undecided
   4   Disagree
   5   Strongly disagree

4. The instructor for the library presentation met with the class for the fully allotted time period.

   1   Strongly agree
   2   Agree
   3   Neutral/Undecided
   4   Disagree
   5   Strongly disagree

5. The instructor handled difficult situations with poise during the library presentation.

    1   Strongly agree

    2   Agree

    3   Neutral/Undecided

    4   Disagree

    5   Strongly disagree

6. The instructor kept the class under control during the library presentation.

    1   Strongly agree

    2   Agree

    3   Neutral/Undecided

    4   Disagree

    5   Strongly disagree

7. The instructor lectured with minimum reliance on notes.

    1   Strongly agree

    2   Agree

    3   Neutral/Undecided

    4   Disagree

    5   Strongly disagree

8. The instructor stayed on the subject.

    1   Strongly agree

    2   Agree

    3   Neutral/Undecided

    4   Disagree

    5   Strongly disagree

9. The instructor adapted easily to changing/unexpected classroom situations.

    1   Strongly agree

    2   Agree

    3   Neutral/Undecided

    4   Disagree

    5   Strongly disagree

10. The instructor varied his/her approach to teaching the subject matter.

    1   Strongly agree
    2   Agree
    3   Neutral/Undecided
    4   Disagree
    5   Strongly disagree

11. The overall effectiveness of the instructor for the library \<blank\> was excellent.

    1   Strongly agree
    2   Agree
    3   Neutral/Undecided
    4   Disagree
    5   Strongly disagree

12. In comparison with other instructors at \<Blank\>, I would rate this instructor as: *(Please check your answer on a scale from 1 to 5 where 1 is the best.)*

    ___ 1
    ___ 2
    ___ 3
    ___ 4
    ___ 5

B. Clarity of Presentation

1. The instructor gave lectures that facilitated taking notes.

    1   Strongly agree
    2   Agree
    3   Neutral/Undecided
    4   Disagree
    5   Strongly disagree

2. When the instructor wrote on the board during the library presentation, only part of the class could see.

    1   Strongly agree
    2   Agree
    3   Neutral/Undecided
    4   Disagree
    5   Strongly disagree

3. The instructor summarized major points.

    1   Strongly agree
    2   Agree
    3   Neutral/Undecided
    4   Disagree
    5   Strongly disagree

4. The instructor for the library <blank> explained the subject matter clearly.

    1   Strongly agree
    2   Agree
    3   Neutral/Undecided
    4   Disagree
    5   Strongly disagree

5. The instructor adequately defined new terms and concepts.

    1   Strongly agree
    2   Agree
    3   Neutral/Undecided
    4   Disagree
    5   Strongly disagree

6. The instructor made the session relevant to my need by showing implications and applications.

    1   Strongly agree
    2   Agree
    3   Neutral/Undecided
    4   Disagree
    5   Strongly disagree

7. The instructor used relevant examples of applications for the skills and concepts covered.

   1 Strongly agree

   2 Agree

   3 Neutral/Undecided

   4 Disagree

   5 Strongly disagree

8. The instructor gave references for the most difficult points.

   1 Strongly agree

   2 Agree

   3 Neutral/Undecided

   4 Disagree

   5 Strongly disagree

9. The instructor of the library <blank> explained the purpose and scope of the session clearly.

   1 Strongly agree

   2 Agree

   3 Neutral/Undecided

   4 Disagree

   5 Strongly disagree

10. The instructor explained the relationship between the content of the library presentation and my assignment.

    1 Strongly agree

    2 Agree

    3 Neutral/Undecided

    4 Disagree

    5 Strongly disagree

11. The instructor used terms that I could understand to explain the subject matter.

    1 Strongly agree

    2 Agree

    3 Neutral/Undecided

    4 Disagree

    5 Strongly disagree

12. The instructor used terms and expressions suitable for the level of the audience of the <blank>.

    1   Strongly agree

    2   Agree

    3   Neutral/Undecided

    4   Disagree

    5   Strongly disagree

13. The instructor of the library <blank> had effective communication and presentation skills.

    1   Strongly agree

    2   Agree

    3   Neutral/Undecided

    4   Disagree

    5   Strongly disagree

C. Preparation and Organization

1. The instructor for the library <blank> was not well prepared.

    1   Strongly agree

    2   Agree

    3   Neutral/Undecided

    4   Disagree

    5   Strongly disagree

2. The instructor presented well-prepared lectures and learning activities.

    1   Strongly agree

    2   Agree

    3   Neutral/Undecided

    4   Disagree

    5   Strongly disagree

3. The instructor for the library <blank> was not well organized.

    1   Strongly agree

    2   Agree

    3   Neutral/Undecided

    4   Disagree

    5   Strongly disagree

4. The instructor presented subject matter in a clear, understandable, and organized manner.

1 Strongly agree
2 Agree
3 Neutral/Undecided
4 Disagree
5 Strongly disagree

D. Teaching Methods

1. The instructor encouraged discussion.

1 Strongly agree
2 Agree
3 Neutral/Undecided
4 Disagree
5 Strongly disagree

2. The instructor effectively facilitated class discussion.

1 Strongly agree
2 Agree
3 Neutral/Undecided
4 Disagree
5 Strongly disagree

3. The instructor effectively presented and explained ideas.

1 Strongly agree
2 Agree
3 Neutral/Undecided
4 Disagree
5 Strongly disagree

4. The instructor answered questions clearly and concisely.

1 Strongly agree
2 Agree
3 Neutral/Undecided
4 Disagree
5 Strongly disagree

5. The instructor adapted his/her teaching methods to address the learning difficulties/styles of students.

    1   Strongly agree

    2   Agree

    3   Neutral/Undecided

    4   Disagree

    5   Strongly disagree

E.   Knowledge of Classroom Assignments

1. The instructor was knowledgeable about my assignment.

    1   Strongly agree

    2   Agree

    3   Neutral/Undecided

    4   Disagree

    5   Strongly disagree

2. The instructor was knowledgeable about the library materials s/he discussed.

    1   Strongly agree

    2   Agree

    3   Neutral/Undecided

    4   Disagree

    5   Strongly disagree

3. The instructor stimulated my interest in library material that will help me complete my classroom assignment.

    1   Strongly agree

    2   Agree

    3   Neutral/Undecided

    4   Disagree

    5   Strongly disagree

4. The instructor was enthusiastic about teaching the library material related to my classroom assignment.

    1   Strongly agree

    2   Agree

    3   Neutral/Undecided

    4   Disagree

    5   Strongly disagree

5. The instructor was knowledgeable about how the library materials discussed related to my class assignment.

    1   Strongly agree

    2   Agree

    3   Neutral/Undecided

    4   Disagree

    5   Strongly disagree

6. The instructor presented up-to-date library material on my classroom assignment.

    1   Strongly agree

    2   Agree

    3   Neutral/Undecided

    4   Disagree

    5   Strongly disagree

7. The instructor was able to clarify how the use of library materials related to my class assignment.

    1   Strongly agree

    2   Agree

    3   Neutral/Undecided

    4   Disagree

    5   Strongly disagree

8. The instructor was able to answer questions about library materials covered in the <blank>.

    1   Strongly agree

    2   Agree

    3   Neutral/Undecided

    4   Disagree

    5   Strongly disagree

F.   Interactions with Students/Participants

1. The instructor was willing to help participants in the library <blank>.

    1   Strongly agree

    2   Agree

    3   Neutral/Undecided

    4   Disagree

    5   Strongly disagree

2. The instructor motivated library <blank> participants to learn.

    1   Strongly agree

    2   Agree

    3   Neutral/Undecided

    4   Disagree

    5   Strongly disagree

3. The instructor was approachable.

    1   Strongly agree

    2   Agree

    3   Neutral/Undecided

    4   Disagree

    5   Strongly disagree

4. The instructor encouraged independent and critical thinking.

    1   Strongly agree

    2   Agree

    3   Neutral/Undecided

    4   Disagree

    5   Strongly disagree

5. The instructor encouraged participant initiative.

    1   Strongly agree

    2   Agree

    3   Neutral/Undecided

    4   Disagree

    5   Strongly disagree

6. The instructor/media specialist stimulated my sense of personal involvement in library resources and search strategies.

    1   Strongly agree
    2   Agree
    3   Neutral/Undecided
    4   Disagree
    5   Strongly disagree

7. The instructor was willing to review material from prior classes.

    1   Strongly agree
    2   Agree
    3   Neutral/Undecided
    4   Disagree
    5   Strongly disagree

8. The instructor encouraged participants to ask questions and to make relevant comments.

    1   Strongly agree
    2   Agree
    3   Neutral/Undecided
    4   Disagree
    5   Strongly disagree

9. The instructor was considerate of participants' opinions.

    1   Strongly agree
    2   Agree
    3   Neutral/Undecided
    4   Disagree
    5   Strongly disagree

10. The instructor discussed points of view other than his/her own.

    1   Strongly agree
    2   Agree
    3   Neutral/Undecided
    4   Disagree
    5   Strongly disagree

11. The instructor invited criticism of his/her own ideas.

    1   Strongly agree
    2   Agree
    3   Neutral/Undecided
    4   Disagree
    5   Strongly disagree

12. The instructor invited participants to share their knowledge and experience.

    1   Strongly agree
    2   Agree
    3   Neutral/Undecided
    4   Disagree
    5   Strongly disagree

13. The instructor encouraged cooperative working and learning among participants.

    1   Strongly agree
    2   Agree
    3   Neutral/Undecided
    4   Disagree
    5   Strongly disagree

14. The instructor was impartial in dealings with students.

    1   Strongly agree
    2   Agree
    3   Neutral/Undecided
    4   Disagree
    5   Strongly disagree

15. The instructor was sensitive to participants' feelings and problems.

    1   Strongly agree
    2   Agree
    3   Neutral/Undecided
    4   Disagree
    5   Strongly disagree

16. The instructor showed respect to all participants.

  1 Strongly agree
  2 Agree
  3 Neutral/Undecided
  4 Disagree
  5 Strongly disagree

17. The instructor was sensitive to individual student differences.

  1 Strongly agree
  2 Agree
  3 Neutral/Undecided
  4 Disagree
  5 Strongly disagree

G. Personal Characteristics and Mannerisms

1. The instructor was dynamic and energetic.

  1 Strongly agree
  2 Agree
  3 Neutral/Undecided
  4 Disagree
  5 Strongly disagree

2. The instructor was calm and relaxed.

  1 Strongly agree
  2 Agree
  3 Neutral/Undecided
  4 Disagree
  5 Strongly disagree

3. The instructor was tense and nervous.

  1 Strongly agree
  2 Agree
  3 Neutral/Undecided
  4 Disagree
  5 Strongly disagree

4. The instructor showed a sense of humor.

    1   Strongly agree

    2   Agree

    3   Neutral/Undecided

    4   Disagree

    5   Strongly disagree

5. The instructor was friendly.

    1   Strongly agree

    2   Agree

    3   Neutral/Undecided

    4   Disagree

    5   Strongly disagree

6. The instructor was concerned and helpful.

    1   Strongly agree

    2   Agree

    3   Neutral/Undecided

    4   Disagree

    5   Strongly disagree

7. The instructor was free of distracting or annoying mannerisms.

    1   Strongly agree

    2   Agree

    3   Neutral/Undecided

    4   Disagree

    5   Strongly disagree

8. The instructor maintained good eye contact with participants.

    1   Strongly agree

    2   Agree

    3   Neutral/Undecided

    4   Disagree

    5   Strongly disagree

9. The instructor repeated him/herself excessively.

  1 Strongly agree

  2 Agree

  3 Neutral/Undecided

  4 Disagree

  5 Strongly disagree

10. The instructor spoke <u>too</u> fast.

  1 Strongly agree

  2 Agree

  3 Neutral/Undecided

  4 Disagree

  5 Strongly disagree

11. The instructor spoke in a clear and distinct voice.

  1 Strongly agree

  2 Agree

  3 Neutral/Undecided

  4 Disagree

  5 Strongly disagree

12. The instructor used distracting expressions such as "okay," "uh," "you know," and "like" excessively.

  1 Strongly agree

  2 Agree

  3 Neutral/Undecided

  4 Disagree

  5 Strongly disagree

13. The instructor varied the speed and tone of his/her voice.

  1 Strongly agree

  2 Agree

  3 Neutral/Undecided

  4 Disagree

  5 Strongly disagree

II. The Teaching Assistant

1. The teaching assistant had good knowledge of course materials.

    1   Strongly agree

    2   Agree

    3   Neutral/Undecided

    4   Disagree

    5   Strongly disagree

2. The teaching assistant was enthusiastic about teaching.

    1   Strongly agree

    2   Agree

    3   Neutral/Undecided

    4   Disagree

    5   Strongly disagree

3. The teaching assistant maintained good rapport with students.

    1   Strongly agree

    2   Agree

    3   Neutral/Undecided

    4   Disagree

    5   Strongly disagree

III. The Instructor of Multiple-Session Library Courses

1. The instructor was present for all of the class sessions.

    1   Strongly agree

    2   Agree

    3   Neutral/Undecided

    4   Disagree

    5   Strongly disagree

2. The instructor's office hours were convenient.

    1   Strongly agree
    2   Agree
    3   Neutral/Undecided
    4   Disagree
    5   Strongly disagree

3. The instructor was available for consultation during office hours and appointments.

    1   Strongly agree
    2   Agree
    3   Neutral/Undecided
    4   Disagree
    5   Strongly disagree

4. The instructor should continue to have office hours.

    1   Strongly agree
    2   Agree
    3   Neutral/Undecided
    4   Disagree
    5   Strongly disagree

5. The instructor's policies for grading and attendance were fair.

    1   Strongly agree
    2   Agree
    3   Neutral/Undecided
    4   Disagree
    5   Strongly disagree

6. The instructor distributed course requirements and policies at the beginning of the <semester/quarter>.

    1   Strongly agree
    2   Agree
    3   Neutral/Undecided
    4   Disagree
    5   Strongly disagree

7. The instructor's syllabus clearly stated important course information, such as grading policy and attendance.

       1   Strongly agree

       2   Agree

       3   Neutral/Undecided

       4   Disagree

       5   Strongly disagree

8. The instructor's course outline clearly stated requirements and due dates for readings, assignments, and papers.

       1   Strongly agree

       2   Agree

       3   Neutral/Undecided

       4   Disagree

       5   Strongly disagree

9. The instructor clearly stated course objectives.

       1   Strongly agree

       2   Agree

       3   Neutral/Undecided

       4   Disagree

       5   Strongly disagree

10. The instructor clearly stated the course's purpose and scope.

       1   Strongly agree

       2   Agree

       3   Neutral/Undecided

       4   Disagree

       5   Strongly disagree

11. The instructor asked for student input.

       1   Strongly agree

       2   Agree

       3   Neutral/Undecided

       4   Disagree

       5   Strongly disagree

12. The instructor related test content to subjects covered in class.

    1   Strongly agree
    2   Agree
    3   Neutral/Undecided
    4   Disagree
    5   Strongly disagree

13. The instructor provided thorough explanations for each section of material that was covered.

    1   Strongly agree
    2   Agree
    3   Neutral/Undecided
    4   Disagree
    5   Strongly disagree

14. The instructor engaged the class interest through meaningful presentations, assignments, and activities.

    1   Strongly agree
    2   Agree
    3   Neutral/Undecided
    4   Disagree
    5   Strongly disagree

15. The instructor was receptive to independent thinking (within the limits of course structure).

    1   Strongly agree
    2   Agree
    3   Neutral/Undecided
    4   Disagree
    5   Strongly disagree

16. The instructor encouraged students to ask questions both in and outside of class.

    1   Strongly agree
    2   Agree
    3   Neutral/Undecided
    4   Disagree
    5   Strongly disagree

17. The instructor provided helpful answers both in and outside of class.

    1   Strongly agree

    2   Agree

    3   Neutral/Undecided

    4   Disagree

    5   Strongly disagree

18. The instructor kept me well informed about my progress in the class.

    1   Strongly agree

    2   Agree

    3   Neutral/Undecided

    4   Disagree

    5   Strongly disagree

19. The instructor provided adequate feedback on my progress.

    1   Strongly agree

    2   Agree

    3   Neutral/Undecided

    4   Disagree

    5   Strongly disagree

20. The instructor made enough comments on my assignments and exams to aid in improving my work.

    1   Strongly agree

    2   Agree

    3   Neutral/Undecided

    4   Disagree

    5   Strongly disagree

21. The instructor returned my work in a reasonable period of time.

    1   Strongly agree

    2   Agree

    3   Neutral/Undecided

    4   Disagree

    5   Strongly disagree

IV. Quality of the Instructor: Open-Ended Questions

1. What advice would you give this instructor (positive and negative) to improve his/her library presentation skills? Be as thorough and specific as you wish.

2. Describe the instructor's skills or qualities that contributed to your learning experience.

3. List any suggestions you have that would enable the instructor to improve his or her teaching of this library presentation.

4. Is there anything you would like to add about your instructor's handling of the library presentation?

5. How has the instructor helped you to learn effectively the subject matter covered in the library presentation?

6. What might the instructor do to help students in future library presentations to learn the subject matter more effectively?

7. Which of the following phrases describe your feelings about the presentation given to your class? (*Please check those that apply.*)

   ____ relevant to student term paper assignments
   ____ not relevant to student term paper assignments
   ____ attempted too much
   ____ too hurried
   ____ not enough was covered

   Comments:

SECTION 13
Summative Evaluation

"Summative" evaluation comes at the end of instruction. It is designed to determine the extent to which instructional objectives have been met.[1] Most often considered as an evaluation for assigning grades, summative evaluation is also conducted to evaluate teaching effectiveness. This section demonstrates ways for library instructors to review their course objectives and instructional success by eliciting responses from student and faculty participants.

Also covered in this section are ways to measure attitudes toward learning. Complementing measurement of learning and equally essential, attitude measurement attempts to appraise the willingness of a student to:

receive, or attend to the instruction given;

respond, or participate in the learning process; and

value, or attach worth to the unit taught.[2]

Information gathered about student attitudes can assist instructors in making needed adjustments to assignments, textbooks, examinations, course lectures, and other parts of the teaching process. To attain accurate measurement of students' attitudes, anonymity of responses is essential.

Librarians in all types of libraries and serving a variety of patrons will find these questions to be useful for their evaluation needs. Some of the questions in this section, particularly those regarding grades, are appropriate mainly for school library media specialists and academic librarians. Questions specifically concerning instruction and how students felt about it may be used in a public, special, academic, or school setting. The questions that are most useful for particular settings will be evident.

---

1. Norman E. Gronlund, *Measurement and Evaluation in Teaching,* 5th ed. (New York: Macmillan, 1985), p. 12.

2. Ibid., pp. 418–22; 516.

I. Grade Expectation

1. The grade I expect to receive for this course is: (*Circle one.*)

   A   Auditing
   B   Pass
   C   Don't Know
   D
   F

II. Workload

1. This was a difficult course.

   1   Strongly agree
   2   Agree
   3   Neutral/Undecided
   4   Disagree
   5   Strongly disagree

2. Based on my past experience, the level of difficulty of this course was: (*Check one.*)

   [ ] Very elementary
   [ ] Somewhat elementary
   [ ] Just right
   [ ] Somewhat difficult
   [ ] Very difficult

3. The amount of work required for this course is appropriate for the credit earned.

   1   Strongly agree
   2   Agree
   3   Neutral/Undecided
   4   Disagree
   5   Strongly disagree

4. <u>Too</u> much library work was required for this course.

    1   Strongly agree

    2   Agree

    3   Neutral/Undecided

    4   Disagree

    5   Strongly disagree

5. The time I spent completing the workbook was time well spent.

    1   Strongly agree

    2   Agree

    3   Neutral/Undecided

    4   Disagree

    5   Strongly disagree

6. Compared to the workload in my other courses, the workload in this course was:

    1   very heavy

    2   somewhat heavy

    3   about average

    4   somewhat light

    5   very light

III. Attitudes

1. My attitude toward using the library is more positive because of this <blank>.

    1   Strongly agree

    2   Agree

    3   Neutral/Undecided

    4   Disagree

    5   Strongly disagree

2. I feel I have achieved the course objectives.

    1   Strongly agree

    2   Agree

    3   Neutral/Undecided

    4   Disagree

    5   Strongly disagree

3. The library <blank> will be of little use to me.

    1   Strongly agree

    2   Agree

    3   Neutral/Undecided

    4   Disagree

    5   Strongly disagree

4. The information in this <blank> will be relevant to my course work.

    1   Strongly agree

    2   Agree

    3   Neutral/Undecided

    4   Disagree

    5   Strongly disagree

5. The library <blank> was well organized.

    1   Strongly agree

    2   Agree

    3   Neutral/Undecided

    4   Disagree

    5   Strongly disagree

6. Of the new things I learned, most were useful.

    1   Strongly agree

    2   Agree

    3   Neutral/Undecided

    4   Disagree

    5   Strongly disagree

7. This <blank> has given me an adequate understanding of how the library's facilities and resources are organized.

    1   Strongly agree

    2   Agree

    3   Neutral/Undecided

    4   Disagree

    5   Strongly disagree

8. This <blank> has developed my skills in using library resources.

    1   Strongly agree

    2   Agree

    3   Neutral/Undecided

    4   Disagree

    5   Strongly disagree

9. I would <u>not</u> recommend this course to a friend.

    1   Strongly agree

    2   Agree

    3   Neutral/Undecided

    4   Disagree

    5   Strongly disagree

10. I would recommend this course to a friend.

    1   Strongly agree

    2   Agree

    3   Neutral/Undecided

    4   Disagree

    5   Strongly disagree

11. I preferred to discuss my research-related problems with my classroom instructor rather than the library instructor or the librarians at the reference desk.

    1   Strongly agree

    2   Agree

    3   Neutral/Undecided

    4   Disagree

    5   Strongly disagree

12. I preferred to discuss my research-related problems with my library instructor or the librarians at the reference desk rather than my classroom instructor.

    1   Strongly agree

    2   Agree

    3   Neutral/Undecided

    4   Disagree

    5   Strongly disagree

13. As a result of this <blank>, I have learned something that I consider valuable.

     1   Strongly agree

     2   Agree

     3   Neutral/Undecided

     4   Disagree

     5   Strongly disagree

14. This session fulfilled my expectations about how to use the library.

     1   Strongly agree

     2   Agree

     3   Neutral/Undecided

     4   Disagree

     5   Strongly disagree

15. To me as a student this instruction was:

of little or no value	of some value	of about average value	valuable	very valuable
[ ]	[ ]	[ ]	[ ]	[ ]

IV. Confidence

1. I feel confident that I can use the <blank> to meet my information needs.

     1   Strongly agree

     2   Agree

     3   Neutral/Undecided

     4   Disagree

     5   Strongly disagree

2. I do not feel comfortable asking for help in the library.

     1   Strongly agree

     2   Agree

     3   Neutral/Undecided

     4   Disagree

     5   Strongly disagree

3. Knowing how to use the library can give a student confidence.

    1   Strongly agree

    2   Agree

    3   Neutral/Undecided

    4   Disagree

    5   Strongly disagree

4. I feel more confident doing library research as a result of <blank>.

    1   Strongly agree

    2   Agree

    3   Neutral/Undecided

    4   Disagree

    5   Strongly disagree

5. Learning to use the library resources efficiently can help me be a better student.

    1   Strongly agree

    2   Agree

    3   Neutral/Undecided

    4   Disagree

    5   Strongly disagree

6. I believe I now have a better understanding of how information is organized and how to access it.

    1   Strongly agree

    2   Agree

    3   Neutral/Undecided

    4   Disagree

    5   Strongly disagree

7. I felt free to ask questions and to disagree with the library <blank> instructor.

    1   Strongly agree

    2   Agree

    3   Neutral/Undecided

    4   Disagree

    5   Strongly disagree

8. The main goal of this library session was to make you aware of the information resources that can enable you to complete your present research assignment.

I feel that this library session met this goal:

    1   Strongly agree
    2   Agree
    3   Neutral/Undecided
    4   Disagree
    5   Strongly disagree

9. I feel the quality of my research paper/project improved as a result of the library instruction session.

    1   Strongly agree
    2   Agree
    3   Neutral/Undecided
    4   Disagree
    5   Strongly disagree

V. Effects of Instruction

1. Before the <blank>, I had very little interest in this subject.

    1   Strongly agree
    2   Agree
    3   Neutral/Undecided
    4   Disagree
    5   Strongly disagree

2. After the <blank>, I had more interest in this subject.

    1   Strongly agree
    2   Agree
    3   Neutral/Undecided
    4   Disagree
    5   Strongly disagree

3. I feel that I could apply the research process outlined in the <blank> to research for other courses.

    1   Strongly agree

    2   Agree

    3   Neutral/Undecided

    4   Disagree

    5   Strongly disagree

4. I feel that this <blank> was practical and will be useful to me in my educational program.

    1   Strongly agree

    2   Agree

    3   Neutral/Undecided

    4   Disagree

    5   Strongly disagree

5. I would choose this instructor again.

    1   Strongly agree

    2   Agree

    3   Neutral/Undecided

    4   Disagree

    5   Strongly disagree

6. My overall rating of this session is: (*Circle one number.*)

    Excellent   1 ——— 2 ——— 3 ——— 4 ——— 5 Poor

7. I would rate the overall value of this session to me as:

    ___ Excellent ___ Good ___ Satisfactory ___ Fair ___ Poor

8. Do you think this session will be of value to you in your studies? Why? or Why not?

9. Have you used the library for any other classes since doing the <blank> project?

Yes ___ No ___

If you answered "Yes" to above question, did the research skills you learned help you with other projects? (*Circle one.*)

Definitely yes				Definitely no
1	2	3	4	5

VI. Questions for Teachers/Faculty

1. I will continue to schedule library sessions for my classes.

1 Strongly agree
2 Agree
3 Neutral/Undecided
4 Disagree
5 Strongly disagree

2. I would recommend this service to other faculty members in my department/school.

1 Strongly agree
2 Agree
3 Neutral/Undecided
4 Disagree
5 Strongly disagree

3. Student assignments showed increasing use of library resources.

1 Strongly agree
2 Agree
3 Neutral/Undecided
4 Disagree
5 Strongly disagree

4. The library instruction class served the purpose that I intended for my students.

        1   Strongly agree

        2   Agree

        3   Neutral/Undecided

        4   Disagree

        5   Strongly disagree

5. Please rate your level of general satisfaction with the library instruction your students received. (*Circle one.*)

        High   1   2   3   4   5   Low

6. Overall, this session provided a valuable learning experience for my students.

        1   Strongly agree

        2   Agree

        3   Neutral/Undecided

        4   Disagree

        5   Strongly disagree

7. I would rate the overall value of this session to my students as:

        ___   Excellent

        ___   Good

        ___   Satisfactory

        ___   Fair

        ___   Poor

SECTION 14
Suggestions, Comments, and Closing Statements

Depending on the scope of your evaluation, you may want to add a question or two asking for general comments about the overall effectiveness of your instruction session. Some of these questions have fixed responses; others ask for open-ended evaluative comments. Although not every respondent will answer questions requesting subjective evaluation, such questions can elicit suggestions for improvement that prove helpful in planning for future instruction. Conversely, if the evaluation questionnaire does not request general comments, respondents will answer only what you have asked, even if they have valuable ideas to share. If you seek additional information about some particular aspect of the class or workshop, prompt for that information in your request for comments. Be sure to leave ample space for answers or provide an additional sheet of paper. Small spaces encourage short answers.

Also included in this section are some sample closing statements. Ending your form with a "thank you" statement imparts a positive feeling to your questionnaire.

OUTLINE OF SECTION 14

Suggestions, Comments, and Closing Statements

I. Evaluation

II. General Comments

III. Suggestions for the Future

IV. Faculty/Classroom Teacher Comments

V. Thank You Statements

I. Evaluation

1. If possible, please list (at least) three things that were done well in this <session, workshop>.

2. If possible, please list (at least) three things that should be changed or improved in this <session, workshop>.

3. What are the major strengths of this session?

    a)
    b)

   What are the major weaknesses?

    a)
    b)

4. What was the most helpful aspect of the library instruction session?

   What was the least helpful?

5. What suggestions do you have for improving the session?

6. If the course had been taught once a week for the entire semester, would you have considered it too much work for one hour of credit?

    ___ Yes
    ___ No
    ___ Don't know

7. What did you particularly like about the session in terms of either the content or the presentation?

8. What would have made the session more relevant to your needs?

9. What library resources were not explained that you would like to know about, or found out about on your own?

10. Would you have preferred:

    ___ that the course be taught by one instructor?
    ___ that the course be taught by several instructors?

11. Would you change this session if you could?

    ___ Yes
    ___ No

    If yes, in what way? _____

12. Should any part of the workshop/presentation be dropped in the future?

13. Did the presentation include unnecessary information?

    ___ Yes
    ___ No

    If yes, what? _____

14. Rate the following two items from A to E, with A being the highest rating, C average, and E the lowest.

    My overall evaluation of the course is: _____
    My overall evaluation of the instructor is: _____

15. On a scale from 1 to 5, with 1 being excellent and 5 being poor, I would rate this program: (*Circle one.*)

        a)   1

        b)   2

        c)   3

        d)   4

        e)   5

16. Please complete the following statements:

Based on this workshop I will be able to:

The questions I still have are:

17. Did the class fulfill your expectations?

    ___ Yes

    ___ No

    ___ Didn't have any expectations

18. Was there anything in particular that you hoped would be covered in the session, but was not?

    ___ Yes

    ___ No

If yes, please note: _____

19. Were all of your questions answered to your satisfaction?

    ___ Yes

    ___ No

    ___ Didn't have any questions

If no, please leave your name and phone number so that we may contact you.

_____

20. What one change would you recommend to make this introduction to research more useful to other students?

21. Would you like to have had more time available for class discussion?

    ___ Yes
    ___ No

22. Were any parts of the presentation/tour confusing?

    ___ Yes
    ___ No

    If yes, please explain briefly.

23. Do you feel this session should be continued as a required part of the General Education Program?

    ___ Yes
    ___ No
    ___ Don't know

    Is there a unit that should be eliminated?

    ___ Yes
    ___ No

    If yes, which one(s)? _____

    Should another unit be added?

    ___ Yes
    ___ No

    If yes, what subject? _____

    Should any of the units be expanded to cover more detail or more sources?

    ___ Yes
    ___ No

    If yes, which one(s)? _____

II. General Comments

1. The following space is provided for any additional comments you wish to make that you feel might assist the instructor in improving this course and teaching performance.

2. Comments or suggestions:

3. We really are interested in the student's perspective; please use the remaining space for any additional comments or suggestions.

4. Optional: Comments/Questions . . . about the library orientation program . . . library services . . . library facilities . . . or library personnel. (Please give your name and phone number if you would like a personal response to your question[s].)

5. Do you have any other comments about the library instruction or the library in general?

III. Suggestions for the Future

1. In what areas, of interest to you, might the library want to build training programs?

2. What questions do you still have about doing research in the library?

3. Are there other aspects of the library that you would like to see addressed in future instruction?

4. Are there other services of this sort that you would like the library to offer?

IV. Faculty/Classroom Teacher Comments

1. We appreciate your support for and participation in our Library Instruction Program. We are constantly striving to improve the content of our presentations. If you have received significant feedback from your students, or if you have comments about the library instruction at <Blank>, would you please take a few moments to let us know? You may write your comments on the bottom of this sheet and mail them back to me at <Address>.

    <blank>   Phone
    <blank>   e-mail

2. We hope this class has met your students' information and research needs. What do you think was the most useful segment of this class?

    What should have been omitted?

3. What can be done to ensure a better presentation next time? (Examples: librarian's better understanding of the assignment, timing of the class during the semester, information or materials that the students need ahead of time.)

4. What else could have been done during this or other library instruction sessions that would assist your classes?

V. Thank You Statements

1. **THANK YOU.**
   Remember that the library staff is available to help you. You may stop at the Reference Desk, or <call our Reference phone/e-mail our Reference address> for help.

2. Thank you for your input.

3. THANK YOU for your cooperation in completing this questionnaire.

4. THANK YOU for helping us evaluate our services by filling out this questionnaire.

<Date>

Dear Library Patron:

Anytown Public Library wishes to determine our patrons'
satisfaction with our new online catalog. If you would like to help us
with our survey, please complete this questionnaire. You may return it to
the box at the Circulation Desk, or mail it to:

Joan Davis
Director, Anytown Public Library
55 E. Main Street
Anytown, CA 90000

In order that we may have time to assess responses, all surveys
should be received by us by October 1, 1995.

Joan Davis
Director, Anytown Public Library
131-8978
e-mail: davis@library.anytown.org

B

Attitude and Measurement Scales

A crucial part of survey research is the design of the survey itself, especially the structure of the questions and the methods of response. Both affect the quality of the data gathered. Methods of response can include: opposite alternatives (yes and no, true and false, approve and disapprove); checklists or cafeteria lists of items (check all that apply: magazines, journals, newspapers); ranking of items (place 1 beside "most important," place 2 beside "important"); and, quantity, rating, or intensity scales. These intensity scales pro-vide respondents with a structured range for indicating attitudes, opinions, interest levels, agreement, or the frequency with which they undertake an activity.

This appendix shows examples of three-, four-, and five-point scales including some of the most common Likert-scale responses. Also shown are typical formats for numerical scales. Note that occasionally in attitude and measurement scales there is a need for "does not apply" as an additional choice.

These scales read horizontally.

Three-Point scales

Low   Moderate   High

Higher   Same   Lower

Greater   Equal   Less

Definitely   Neutral   Definitely
agree   disagree

Above   Average   Below
average   average

Very often   Occasionally   Never

Required   Encouraged   Not mentioned

Four-Point Scales

Many   Some   Very few   None

Excellent   Good   Fair   Poor

Daily   Weekly   Occasionally   Never

Daily   Weekly   Monthly   Once a semester

Five-Point Scales

Strongly
approve   Approve   Undecided   Disapprove   Strongly
disapprove

Very high   Above average   Average   Below average   Very low

Strongly agree   Agree   Neutral   Disagree   Strongly disagree

Poor   Below average   Average   Above average   Excellent

Very
unmotivated   Moderately
unmotivated   Indifferent   Moderately
motivated   Very
motivated

Always   Usually   Sometimes   Rarely   Never

Very poor   Poor   Fair   Good   Very good

Excellent   Very good   Average   Fair   Poor

Numerical Scales

These scales typically have five or more choices; numerical scales with fewer than five choices offer a narrower range of interpretation and data analysis.

Disagree   Agree
−3   −2   −1   0   +1   +2   +3   Not applicable

Low   High
1   2   3   4   5   6   7   Not applicable

                                         Have no
Knowledgeable   knowledge
7   6   5   4   3   2   1

APPENDIX

C

Pre- and Post-Instruction Checklists

Pre-Presentation Checklist

Post-Presentation Checklist

Librarian's To-Do List

Date: _____

Day: _____

How "ready" are you? Check the appropriate answer that reflects your level of thought or preparation.

Pre-Presentation Checklist

Have you considered?

		Yes	No	N/A
I. Audience				
1.	How many people will be attending?	—	—	—
2.	What is the learning level/grade level of the audience?	—	—	—
3.	Do any audience members have special needs?	—	—	—
4.	What are their expectations for outcomes?	—	—	—
5.	What are the audience goals?	—	—	—
6.	Does audience need a pretest?	—	—	—
7.	Does audience need a posttest?	—	—	—
8.	Is group participation necessary?	—	—	—
9.	Will the group need special instructions?	—	—	—
II. Location				
1.	Must the site be reserved?	—	—	—
2.	Can the area be darkened?	—	—	—
3.	Should the area be rearranged?	—	—	—
4.	Can equipment be used in the area?	—	—	—
5.	Are there any limitations of the area?	—	—	—
6.	Are the acoustics acceptable?	—	—	—
III. Handouts				
1.	Are there handouts available that fit the need of the presentation?	—	—	—
2.	Are there handouts available that fit the need of the audience?	—	—	—
3.	Are the handouts current?	—	—	—
4.	Are the handouts accurate?	—	—	—
5.	How many copies of the handouts are needed?	—	—	—
6.	Are there special duplication needs for the handouts?	—	—	—
7.	Are any special materials needed for the handouts? pencils? scoresheets?	—	—	—
8.	Is there an evaluation available?	—	—	—

IV. Presentation/Content

Yes No N/A

Presentation

1. What learning styles best fit the presentation? ___ ___ ___
2. What are the goals of the presentation? ___ ___ ___
3. What are the educational objectives of the presentation? ___ ___ ___
4. Has a presentation outline been prepared? ___ ___ ___
5. How much time does the presentation take? ___ ___ ___
6. Is an evaluation needed? ___ ___ ___

Content

1. Is content appropriate to audience needs? ___ ___ ___
2. Is content accurate? ___ ___ ___
3. Is content current? ___ ___ ___

V. Teaching/Presentation Aids

1. Is the presentation enhanced by audio/visual aids? ___ ___ ___
2. Have such materials (overheads, flipcharts, software) been prepared previously? ___ ___ ___
3. Are materials current? ___ ___ ___
4. Are materials accurate? ___ ___ ___

VI. Equipment

1. Is equipment needed for the presentation? ___ ___ ___
2. Is equipment appropriate for the content/presentation? ___ ___ ___
3. Must equipment be reserved? ___ ___ ___
4. Are special plugs/cords needed? ___ ___ ___
5. Are extra equipment pieces available (bulbs, etc.)? ___ ___ ___

Date: _____

Day: _____

How did you do? Check the appropriate answers to "evaluate" yourself, based on your observations and experience, and comparing your self-assessment to audience evaluations.

Post-Presentation Checklist

How do you think it went. . . . ?

I. Audience   Yes No N/A

    1. Did you correctly assess the learning level/grade level of the audience?   __ __ __

    2. Were special needs of audience members met?   __ __ __

    3. Were audience expectations met?   __ __ __

    4. Were audience goals realized?   __ __ __

    5. Did your audience need a pretest?   __ __ __

    6. Did your audience need a posttest?   __ __ __

    7. Was the group participation successful?   __ __ __

    8. Did the group need special instructions?   __ __ __

II. Location

    1. Did the site need to be reserved?   __ __ __

    2. Was the area adequately darkened?   __ __ __

    3. Did the area need to be rearranged?   __ __ __

    4. Was the equipment in the area functional?   __ __ __

    5. Did the area have any limitation?   __ __ __

    6. Were the acoustics acceptable?   __ __ __

III. Handouts

    1. Did the available handouts fit the need of the presentation?   __ __ __

    2. Did the available handouts fit the needs of the audience?   __ __ __

    3. Were the handouts current?   __ __ __

    4. Were the handouts accurate?   __ __ __

    5. Were there enough copies of the handout(s)?   __ __ __

    6. Were there duplication problems?   __ __ __

    7. Did you have the special materials needed for the presentation? handouts? pencils? score sheets?   __ __ __

		Yes	No	N/A
IV.	**Presentation/Content**			

Presentation

		Yes	No	N/A
1.	Did the learning style chosen fit the presentation?	—	—	—
2.	Were your goals for the presentation met?	—	—	—
3.	Were the educational objectives of the presentation met?	—	—	—
4.	Was the presentation outline adequate?	—	—	—
5.	Was the presentation the appropriate length?	—	—	—

Content

		Yes	No	N/A
1.	Was the content appropriate to the audience needs?	—	—	—
2.	Was the content accurate?	—	—	—
3.	Was the content current?	—	—	—

V. Teaching Presentation Aids

		Yes	No	N/A
1.	Was the presentation enhanced by the use of audio/visual aids?	—	—	—
2.	Were the materials (overheads, flipcharts, software) adequately prepared?	—	—	—
3.	Were the materials current?	—	—	—
4.	Were the materials accurate?	—	—	—

VI. Equipment

		Yes	No	N/A
1.	Was all equipment functioning?	—	—	—
2.	Was the equipment appropriate for the content/presentation?	—	—	—
3.	Did equipment need to be reserved?	—	—	—
4.	Were special cords/plugs needed?	—	—	—
5.	Were extra equipment pieces available (bulbs, etc.)?	—	—	—

Date: _____

Day: _____

Librarian's To-Do List

1. People to call/Questions to ask

2. Files to check
    (other presentations? documentation?)

3. Items to prepare
    (outlines? overheads?)

4. Areas/Locations to visit
    (machines/software to be used? classroom? theater? library area?)

5. Documents to review
    (handouts available?)

6. Requests to be placed
    (rooms scheduled? duplication orders placed?)

Sample Evaluation: Course-Integrated Instruction

Sample Evaluation: One-Shot Electronic Instruction Session

Sample Evaluation: University Library Faculty Orientation

Sample Evaluation: University Library Student Orientation

Sample Evaluation: Library Orientation for International Students

Sample School Library Media Center Evaluation for Students

Sample School Library Media Center Evaluation for Faculty

Sample Evaluation: General Instruction Programs

Sample Evaluation: Course-Integrated Instruction

The following sample evaluation is intended for academic librarians to administer to faculty members for input regarding the effectiveness of course-integrated instruction. School librarians may want to modify these questions to fit the curriculum and faculty needs of their situation.

FACULTY EVALUATION OF LIBRARY INSTRUCTION

Faculty who request our instruction are seldom asked formally how we can improve upon the library instruction sessions we present. In the case of course-integrated instruction, it is crucial to determine if the level of instruction is appropriate, if the material covered meets the overall goals of the course, and if student work has improved as a result of the instruction. There are also the challenges of team teaching, which course-integrated instruction is, to evaluate and comment upon. For example, if the librarian is grading the library portion of the course assignments, is the same standard for excellence set by the professor being used by the librarian? Did the instruction aid in achievement of the course goals as stated on the syllabus?

	☞	**1.** The library instruction sessions met my expectations for the course level.
		A Strongly agree B Agree C Neutral D Disagree E Strongly disagree
	☞	**2.** The library instructor was well prepared.
		A Strongly agree B Agree C Neutral D Disagree E Strongly disagree
	☞	**3.** The library instructor was knowledgeable.
		A Strongly agree B Agree C Neutral D Disagree E Strongly disagree

		4.	The instruction in library use was too elementary and remedial.

A   Strongly agree
B   Agree
C   Neutral
D   Disagree
E   Strongly disagree

		5.	Students' assignments and papers showed a greater depth in use of source material.

A   Strongly agree
B   Agree
C   Neutral
D   Disagree
E   Strongly disagree

		6.	The library assignments were appropriate for learning library research skills.

A   Strongly agree
B   Agree
C   Neutral
D   Disagree
E   Strongly disagree

		7.	I did not notice a difference in quality of student work regarding use of library resources as a result of the library instruction.

A   Strongly agree
B   Agree
C   Neutral
D   Disagree
E   Strongly disagree

		8.	I would recommend course-integrated library instruction to other faculty members.

A   Strongly agree
B   Agree
C   Neutral
D   Disagree
E   Strongly disagree

Sample Evaluation: One-Shot Electronic Instruction Session

These one-time-only sessions, common in all types of libraries, are used to explain online catalogs, specific CD-ROMs, or electronic indexes. Questions 1 and 2 pertain to an academic setting; all other questions could be used in any library to evaluate effectiveness of the training session.

STUDENT FEEDBACK SHEET

Librarian's Name _____ Date _____

Course Title _____

Please help us by taking a few moments to complete this form. All comments are welcome.

1. Check one:

    ___ Graduate

    ___ Undergraduate

    ___ Other

2. Department or major: _____

3. How often do you use <Blank> Library?

    ___ a) at least once a week

    ___ b) at least twice a month

    ___ c) less than twice a month

    ___ d) have never used

4. Have you ever asked for assistance at the reference desk?

    ___ Yes   ___ No

5. Use the following numbers to indicate your agreement with the following statements:

    1   Strongly agree

    2   Agree

    3   Undecided

    4   Disagree

    5   Strongly disagree

    ___ I know how to use the card catalog.

    ___ I know how to use the CD-ROM journal/magazine and newspaper indexes.

    ___ I know how to use printed indexes.

    ___ I know how to use the online catalog.

    ___ I know how to use computerized indexes.

6. This session has given me adequate understanding of and skill in using the <online catalog/CD-ROM/ <Blank> Database>.

    1   Strongly agree

    2   Agree

    3   Undecided

    4   Disagree

    5   Strongly disagree

7. There was adequate time to ask questions.

    1   Strongly agree

    2   Agree

    3   Undecided

    4   Disagree

    5   Strongly disagree

8. There was enough practice time.

    1   Strongly agree

    2   Agree

    3   Undecided

    4   Disagree

    5   Strongly disagree

9. I feel confident that I can use the <online catalog/CD-ROM/<Blank> Database> to find information for future assignments.

    1   Strongly agree

    2   Agree

    3   Undecided

    4   Disagree

    5   Strongly disagree

10. Was there anything in particular that you hoped would be covered in the session, but was not?

    ___ Yes   ___ No

    If yes, please note: _____

11. Do you feel that you need further instruction in using the <online catalog/CD-ROM/<Blank>Database>?

    ___ Yes   ___ No

12. We are really interested in the student's perspective: please use the remaining space for any additional comments or suggestions.

THANK YOU for helping us evaluate our services by filling out this questionnaire.

Sample Evaluation: University Library Faculty Orientation

Using SCHOLAR As a Teaching Tool

To better serve the needs of instructors teaching entry level English courses, the References and Instructional Services Department at Parks Library wishes to evaluate the orientation session you attended earlier this semester. Please help us by taking a few moments to complete this evaluation.

For each of the following statements, designate your choice by filling in the space(s) for the corresponding letter(s).

1. What courses will you be teaching this semester?   A. ENG101; B. ENG104; C. ENG105

2. In general, how often per semester will your course(s) require papers or research projects involving use of the library?   A. Never; B. 1–2; C. 3–4; D. More than 4

Use the following scale to indicate whether you agree or disagree with the statements below.

A. Strongly agree; B. Agree; C. Neutral; D. Disagree; E. Strongly disagree

3. The presentation content was related to my teaching needs.

4. This session gave me adequate understanding of the content and how to use the SCHOLAR catalog.

5. This session gave me adequate understanding of the content and how to use the SCHOLAR indexes.

6. I was able to apply some of the information to my classroom teaching.

7. Guides and materials (handouts) distributed were helpful.

8. It would have been better if there had been time for hands-on practice.

9. The instructor spoke too fast.

10. The instructor had effective presentation skills.

11. The instructor stimulated my interest in using SCHOLAR for teaching.

12. The instructor was enthusiastic about teaching.

COMMENTS OVER!

Printed in U.S.A.   Mark Reflex® by NCS MM100642:321   A1804

Please write your comments in the blank space.

13. What did you find most useful?

14. What should have been included that wasn't?

15. General comments to improve our instruction.

Thank you for your input!

	A	B	C	D	E	F	G	H	I	J
21	①	②	③	④	⑤	⑥	⑦	⑧	⑨	⓪
22	①	②	③	④	⑤	⑥	⑦	⑧	⑨	⓪
23	①	②	③	④	⑤	⑥	⑦	⑧	⑨	⓪
24	①	②	③	④	⑤	⑥	⑦	⑧	⑨	⓪
25	①	②	③	④	⑤	⑥	⑦	⑧	⑨	⓪
26	①	②	③	④	⑤	⑥	⑦	⑧	⑨	⓪
27	①	②	③	④	⑤	⑥	⑦	⑧	⑨	⓪
28	①	②	③	④	⑤	⑥	⑦	⑧	⑨	⓪
29	①	②	③	④	⑤	⑥	⑦	⑧	⑨	⓪
30	①	②	③	④	⑤	⑥	⑦	⑧	⑨	⓪
31	①	②	③	④	⑤	⑥	⑦	⑧	⑨	⓪
32	①	②	③	④	⑤	⑥	⑦	⑧	⑨	⓪
33	①	②	③	④	⑤	⑥	⑦	⑧	⑨	⓪
34	①	②	③	④	⑤	⑥	⑦	⑧	⑨	⓪
35	①	②	③	④	⑤	⑥	⑦	⑧	⑨	⓪
36	①	②	③	④	⑤	⑥	⑦	⑧	⑨	⓪
37	①	②	③	④	⑤	⑥	⑦	⑧	⑨	⓪
38	①	②	③	④	⑤	⑥	⑦	⑧	⑨	⓪
39	①	②	③	④	⑤	⑥	⑦	⑧	⑨	⓪
40	①	②	③	④	⑤	⑥	⑦	⑧	⑨	⓪

Sample Evaluation: University Library Student Orientation

STUDENT FEEDBACK SHEET

To better serve the needs of students whose second language is English, the Reference and Instructional Services Department at Parks Library wishes to evaluate the online catalog and database orientation session given earlier this semester. Please help us by taking a few moments to complete this evaluation form and return it to your instructor.

For each of the following statements, designate your choice by filling in the corresponding letter.

1. My current classification or the level that I will be entering is   A. Undergraduate; B. Master's; C. Ph.D.

2. My major will be/is in the area of: A. Business; B. Science and Related Technologies; C. Humanities; D. Social Sciences; E. Undecided

Use the following scale to indicate how much you agree or disagree with the emaining statements.

A. Strongly agree; B. Agree; C. Neutral; D. Disagree; E. Strongly disagree

3. This session gave me valuable information which I needed to function in the library.

4. The presentation has given me adequate understanding of and skill in using the online catalog (ICAT).

5. The presentation has given me adequate understanding of and skill in using the index databases.

6. The print materials (handouts) were useful.

7. The information was appropriately presented for my level of English skill.

8. The presentation was appropriate for my level of education.

9. Too much information was given at the library presentation.

10. The material was presented at an appropriate pace.

11. There was enough time for hands-on practice during the session.

12. The instructor had effective communication and presentation skills.

13. Would you change this session if you could?   A. Yes; B. No

   If "Yes," in what way?   (*Please write on back of evaluation sheet.*)

Thank you for your input!

Sample Evaluation: Library Orientation for International Students

STUDENT EVALUATION OF LIBRARY ORIENTATION

To better serve the needs of international students, the References and Instructional Services Department at Parks Library wishes to evaluate the orientation tour you just attended.

Please take a few moments to answer the following questions.

1. What is your home country?   (*Please write.*) _____

2. What is your age?   (*Circle.*)

   A.   22 years or under   D.   33–37 years
   B.   23–27 years   E.   Over 37 years
   C.   28–32 years

3. What degree will you be studying for at Iowa State?   (*Circle.*)

   A.   BS   B.   MS   C.   PhD

4. What is your previous library experience in your home country?   (*Circle all that apply.*)

   A.   Public or city library
   B.   High school library or equivalent (i.e., secondary school)
   C.   College or other university library
   D.   Other (Please specify) _____

5. Do you have experience using other university libraries in the United States?

   A.   Yes = > If yes, where? _____
   B.   No

Use the following scale to indicate whether you agree or disagree with the statements below.

   A. Strongly agree;   B. Agree;   C. Neutral;   D. Disagree;   E. Strongly disagree

6. The tour of the Library was very helpful for my
   understanding of the location of specific library
   services, collections, and facilities.   A__   B__   C__   D__   E__

7. The tour leader spoke too fast.   A__   B__   C__   D__   E__

8. The tour group was too large.   A__   B__   C__   D__   E__

9. What is the most important thing you learned on the tour?   (*Please write.*)

_____

_____

Sample School Library Media Center Evaluation for Students

\<BLANK> HIGH SCHOOL LIBRARY MEDIA CENTER

Your opinion matters! The purpose of this questionnaire is to find out your opinions about the class you just attended. The questionnaire assesses your opinion about what this class is actually like. Please answer all questions honestly to help me help you. Your answers will be confidential.

Directions: Please write the letter of your answer, from the choices below, next to each question.

          A   Strongly agree
          B   Agree
          C   Neutral/Undecided
          D   Disagree
          E   Strongly disagree

____ **1.** The purpose of the library class was clear.

____ **2.** The content of the library class I attended was excellent.

____ **3.** There were enough seats and handouts for all students.

____ **4.** The librarian effectively presented and explained ideas.

____ **5.** The instructor answered questions clearly and concisely.

____ **6.** The instructor was knowledgeable about my assignment.

____ **7.** The instructor stimulated my interest in library material that will help me complete my classroom assignment.

____ **8.** As a result of the presentation, I understand how to use indexes to find periodical articles on my subject.

____ **9.** As a result of the presentation, I understand how to find the issues of periodicals and newspapers owned by the library.

____ **10.** As a result of the presentation, I understand how to search the library database(s).

____ **11.** The librarian encouraged discussion.

____ **12.** The librarian did <u>not</u> present the subject matter in a clear, understandable, and organized manner.

Is there anything else you would like me to know? Please write your comments neatly on the back of this evaluation. Return the evaluation in the box on the desk at the front of the room.

THANK YOU!!!

Sample School Library Media Center Evalution for Faculty

<BLANK> MIDDLE SCHOOL LIBRARY MEDIA CENTER

Please help me assess the effectiveness of the library unit with your students. Your answers will help me plan for future instructional sessions.

Directions: Circle one answer.

1. The School Library Media Specialist (SLMS) was well prepared.

    a   Strongly agree

    b   Agree

    c   Neutral/Undecided

    d   Disagree

    e   Strongly disagree

2. The SLMS was knowledgeable.

    a   Strongly agree

    b   Agree

    c   Neutral/Undecided

    d   Disagree

    e   Strongly disagree

3. The SLMS did <u>not</u> use active learning techniques.

    a   Strongly agree

    b   Agree

    c   Neutral/Undecided

    d   Disagree

    e   Strongly disagree

4. The <u>content level</u> of the library presentation was appropriate to the <u>grade level</u> of my assignment.

    a   Strongly agree

    b   Agree

    c   Neutral/Undecided

    d   Disagree

    e   Strongly disagree

5. The library presentation <u>instruction level</u> was appropriate to the <u>grade level</u> of my class.

    a   Strongly agree

    b   Agree

    c   Neutral/Undecided

    d   Disagree

    e   Strongly disagree

6. The overall quality of the library presentation(s) given to my class(es) was excellent.

    a   Strongly agree

    b   Agree

    c   Neutral/Undecided

    d   Disagree

    e   Strongly disagree

7. The teaching format of this library presentation did <u>not</u> address the needs of my students.

    a   Strongly agree

    b   Agree

    c   Neutral/Undecided

    d   Disagree

    e   Strongly disagree

8. The library presentation related to my course objectives as stated by me during my initial meeting with the SLMS.

    a   Strongly agree

    b   Agree

    c   Neutral/Undecided

    d   Disagree

    e   Strongly disagree

9. There were points I wanted covered that were missing from the library presentation.

    a   Strongly agree

    b   Agree

    c   Neutral/Undecided

    d   Disagree

    e   Strongly disagree

10. I did not notice a difference in the quality of student work regarding use of library resources as a result of the library instruction.

    a   Strongly agree

    b   Agree

    c   Neutral/Undecided

    d   Disagree

    e   Strongly disagree

Please write any comments on a separate sheet or make an appointment with me to talk about specific points. Thank you for your time!

Sample Evaluation: General Instructional Programs

\<BLANK\> PUBLIC LIBRARY WORKSHOP EVALUATION

To better meet the needs of those who attend our instruction programs and workshops, the \<Blank\> Public Library wishes you to evaluate the session you just attended. Please help us by taking a few moments to complete this evaluation. All answers will be confidential.

Directions: Using a pen or pencil and writing legibly, please give us answers to the following questions.

Program title:

Date:

So we know who attends our sessions, please tell us your:

Sex: Male   Female

Age:

How far did you travel to attend this session (approximately)?

How often do you use the library (e.g., daily, weekly, monthly, etc.)?

I found out about this session from: (*Please circle all that apply.*)

1. a radio announcement
2. newspaper
3. cable TV program
4. flyer
5. a friend
6. librarian
7. other (please name)

Please circle one answer for each of the following questions.

1. The librarian was well prepared.

    a) Strongly agree
    b) Agree
    c) Neutral/Undecided
    d) Disagree
    e) Strongly disagree

2. The librarian presented the material in a clear, understandable, and organized manner.

    a) Strongly agree

    b) Agree

    c) Neutral/Undecided

    d) Disagree

    e) Strongly disagree

3. The librarian did <u>not</u> speak in a loud and clear voice.

    a) Strongly agree

    b) Agree

    c) Neutral/Undecided

    d) Disagree

    e) Strongly disagree

4. This workshop was an excellent way to learn <the OPAC, Internet, Resources on Job Hunting>.

    a) Strongly agree

    b) Agree

    c) Neutral/Undecided

    d) Disagree

    e) Strongly disagree

5. As a result of this library presentation, I now understand how to <presentation topic>.

    a) Strongly agree

    b) Agree

    c) Neutral/Undecided

    d) Disagree

    e) Strongly disagree

6. Is there any thing else you would like to tell us? Please write your comments below.

Thank you for your cooperation in completing this questionnaire. Please return it to the box marked "Evaluations" at the Circulation Desk.

Glossary

assessment Any technique or instrument used to evaluate students, teachers, or programs both for strengths or weaknesses.

attitude scale Any of a series of attitude indices that have quantitative values relative to one another; a type of scale often used to determine the degree of satisfaction with a program or supporting materials.

evaluation The use of research techniques to measure the degree to which identified objectives have been achieved in a program; the process of collecting, analyzing, and interpreting information to determine the adequacy and effectiveness of a program or form of instruction.

focus group Group of five to ten people who, with a moderator, discuss a series of topics or questions for no more than one to two hours to provide useful information and insights to the moderator. The procedure relies primarily on interaction rather than question-and-answer format.

formative evaluation Assessing a program or product during its development or implementation.

goal A nonquantified, long-range, visionary statement of intent.

halo effect Positive bias in ratings arising from the tendency of a rater to be influenced in his/her assessment of specific traits by his/her general impression of the entity being rated or by the previous items in the assessment.

Likert-type scale A test of interests or attitudes in which persons are asked to indicate the extent to which they agree or disagree with a number of statements, usually on a five-point scale; commonly, one end of the scale represents "strongly agree" and the other "strongly disagree."

manual Synonymous with handbook; a book of advice or instructions, often intended to accompany a course.

needs assessment A study to identify the discrepancy between "what is" and "what ought to be"; the first step in formulating the purposes of a new program. A needs assessment should be conducted prior to establishing goals and objectives.

objective An explicitly worded statement specifying a behavior that learners should be able to exhibit in some measurable form. It should specify three aspects: the desired behavior, criteria or standards of quality or quantity, and the conditions under which successful performance of the behavior will occur.

pathfinder A guide to using a particular tool, e.g., CD-ROM, index, online catalog.

posttest Test given at the end of an instruction program to determine the extent to which the learner has achieved specified objectives.

pretest A test given before instruction to measure existing levels of proficiency. Results of a pretest may be compared with those of a posttest to determine how much was learned.

qualitative data Information in the form of words, usually resulting from interviewing or observing and reporting.

quantitative data Information in the form of numbers and quantities to which statistical methods may be applied, usually resulting from counting and measuring.

reliability The extent to which a given question or test will result in a given person or group obtaining the same score on different occasions; the dependability of repeated measures. Usually multiple-choice questions are more reliable than open-ended or essay questions.

search strategy   The development of search statements used to find answers to an inquiry.

statistical methods   Methods of collecting and analyzing quantitative data about a limited number of cases to make sensible and reliable inferences about a wider number of cases.

summative evaluation   Assessment of the overall impact or outcome of a program or product after it has been fully developed and implemented.

survey technique   Systematic collection of information from a representative sample of individuals to make assumptions about the larger population from which the sample was drawn.

trail blazer   A guide to using a particular tool, such as an index, CD-ROM, or online catalog.

validity   The extent to which a test measures what it is intended to measure. A test cannot be valid unless it has high reliability.

workbook   A study or learning guide containing exercises and practice materials for students.

Sources:

Rowntree, Derek. *A Dictionary of Education.* Totowa, N.J.: Barnes and Noble, 1982.

Shafritz, Jay M., Richard P. Koeppe, and Elizabeth W. Soper. *Facts on File Dictionary of Education.* New York: Facts on File, 1988.

Bibliography

Ackerson, Linda G., Jeanne G. Howard, and Virginia E. Young. "Assessing the Relationship between Library Instruction Methods and the Quality of Undergraduate Research." *Research Strategies* 9 (Summer 1991): 139–41.

Adams, Mignon M. "Effects of Evaluation on Teaching Methods." In *Improving Library Instruction: How to Teach and How to Evaluate.* Library Orientation Series, no. 9. Ann Arbor: Pierian Press, 1979.

Adams, Mignon M. "Evaluation." In *Sourcebook for Bibliographic Instruction.* Chicago: American Library Association, 1993.

Adams, Mignon M., Mary Loe, T. Mark Morey, and Robert E. Schell. *Evaluating a Library Instruction Program: A Case Study of Effective Intracampus Cooperation.* Oswego, N.Y.: State University of New York College at Oswego, <1983>. ERIC ED 274378.

Aleamoni, Lawrence M., ed. *Techniques for Evaluating and Improving Instruction.* San Francisco: Jossey-Bass, 1987.

Anderson, James. "Using Projectors." *ECC News* (Educational Communications Center, State University of New York at Buffalo) (January 1990): 25–30.

Association of College and Research Libraries. Bibliographic Instruction Section. Subcommittee on Evaluation. *Evaluating Bibliographic Instruction.* Chicago: American Library Association, 1983.

Association of College and Research Libraries. Bibliographic Instruction Section. *Evaluating Bibliographic Instruction: A Handbook.* Chicago: American Library Association, 1983.

Backlund, Phil. "Using Student Ratings of Faculty in the Instructional Development Process." *ACA Bulletin* 81 (August 1991): 7–12.

Barclay, Donald. "Evaluating Library Instruction: Doing the Best You Can with What You Have." *RQ* 33 (Winter 1993): 195–202.

Basic Information Seeking Competencies: High School to College. Columbus: Academic Library Association of Ohio, Ohio Educational Library/Media Association, Ohio Library Association, 1990. ERIC ED 335054.

Beaudin, Bart P., and Don Quick. *Instructional Video Evaluation.* Fort Collins: Colorado State University, Fort Collins. School of Occupational and Educational Studies, 1993. ERIC ED 366308.

Benefiel, Candace R., and Joe Jaros. "Planning and Testing a Self-Guided Taped Tour in an Academic Library." *RQ* 29 (Winter 1989): 199–207.

Berdie, Douglas R., John F. Anderson, and Marsha A. Niebuhr. *Questionnaires: Design and Use.* 2nd ed. Metuchen, N.J.: Scarecrow Press, 1986.

Bergman, Emily, and Lill Maman. "Aims of User Education: Special Library Results." *Special Libraries* 83 (Summer 1992): 156–62.

Bodi, Sonia. "Collaborating with Faculty in Teaching Critical Thinking: The Role of Librarians." *Research Strategies* 10 (Spring 1992): 69–76.

Brevik, Patricia Senn. *Planning the Library Instruction Program.* Chicago: American Library Association, 1982.

Brottman, May, and May Loe, eds. *The LIRT Library Instruction Handbook.* Englewood, Colo.: Libraries Unlimited, 1990.

Bunge, Charles A. "Factors Related to Output Measures for Reference Services in Public Libraries: Data from Thirty-Six Libraries." *Public Libraries* 29 (January/February 1990): 42–47.

Chen, Ching-chih, ed. *Quantitative Measurement and Dynamic Library Service.* Phoenix: Oryx Press, 1978.

Clark, Alice S., and Kay F. Jones. *Teaching Librarians to Teach: On-the-Job Training for Bibliographic Instruction Librarians.* Metuchen, N.J.: Scarecrow Press, 1986.

Dunkin, Michael J., ed. *The International Encyclopedia of Teaching and Higher Education.* Oxford: Pergamon Press, 1987.

Feinman, Valerie J. "Library Instruction: What Is Our Classroom?" *Computers in Libraries* 14 (February 1994): 33–36.

Frick, Elizabeth. "Evaluating Student Knowledge of Facilities at the University of Colorado, Colorado Springs." In *Improving Library Instruction: How to Teach and How to Evaluate.* Library Orientation Series, no. 9. Ann Arbor: Pierian Press, 1979.

Frick, Elizabeth. "Qualitative Evaluation of User Education Programs: The Best Choice?" *Research Strategies* 8 (Winter 1990): 4–13.

Gebhard, Patricia. "How to Evaluate Library Instructional Programs." *California Librarian* 37 (April 1976): 36–43.

Glazier, Jack D. and Ronald R. Powell. *Qualitative Research in Information Management.* Englewood, Colo.: Libraries Unlimited, 1992.

Greer, Arlene, Lee Watson, and Mary Alom. "Assessment of Learning Outcomes: A Measure of Progress in Library Literacy." *College & Research Libraries* 52 (November 1991): 549–57.

Gronlund, Norman E. *Measurement and Evaluation of Teaching.* 5th ed. New York: Macmillan Publishing, 1985.

Hardesty, Larry, Nicholas P. Lovrich Jr., and James Mannon. "Evaluating Library Use Instruction." *College & Research Libraries* 40 (July 1979): 309–17.

Haws, Rae, Lorna Peterson, and Diana Shonrock. "Survey of Faculty Attitudes towards a Basic Library Skills Course." *College & Research Libraries News* 50 (March 1989): 201–3.

Isbell, Dennis, and Lisa Klammerlocker. "A Formative, Collegial Approach to Evaluating Course-Integrated Instruction." *Research Strategies* 12 (Winter 1994): 24–32.

Jacobson, Gertrude N., and Michael J. Albright. "Motivation Via Videotape: Key to Undergraduate Library Instruction in the Research Library." *Journal of Academic Librarianship* 9 (November 1983): 270–75.

Kulthau, Carol C. "Perceptions of the Information Search Process in Libraries: A Study of Changes from High School through College." *Information Processing and Management* 24 (July/August 1988): 419–27.

Kusack, James M. "Facility Evaluation in Libraries: A Strategy and Methodology for Library Managers." *Library Administration and Management* 7 (Spring 1993): 107–11.

Lawson, V. Lonnie. "Using a Computer-Assisted Instruction Program to Replace the Traditional Library Tour: An Experimental Study." *RQ* 29 (Fall 1989): 71–79.

Lawton, Bethany. "Library Instruction Needs Assessment: Designing Survey Instruments." *Research Strategies* 7 (Summer 1989): 119–28.

Lester, Linda L. *Faculty Perceptions of Students' Knowledge and Use of Libraries.* Charlottesville, Va.: University of Virginia. Alderman Library, 1984. ERIC ED 247949.

Macakanja, Richard. "Creating Visual Presentation Materials." *ECC News* (January 1990): 24–25.

Mellon, Constance A., ed. *Bibliographic Instruction: The Second Generation.* Littleton, Colo.: Libraries Unlimited, 1987.

Nahl-Jakobovits, Diane, and Leon A. Jakobovits. "Bibliographic Instructional Design for Information Literacy: Integrating Affective and Cognitive Objectives." *Research Strategies* 11 (Spring 1993): 73–88.

Olevnik, Peter P. "Evaluation as a Tool for Program Development." In *Improving Library Instruction: How to Teach and How to Evaluate.* Library Orientation Series, no. 9. Ann Arbor: Pierian Press, 1979.

Palmour, Vernon E., Marcia C. Bellassai, and Nancy V. DeWath. *A Planning Process for Public Libraries.* Chicago: American Library Association, 1980.

Pearson, Penelope, and Virginia Tiefel. "Evaluating Undergraduate Library Instruction at the Ohio State University." *Journal of Academic Librarianship* 7 (January 1982): 351–57.

Person, Roland. "Long-Term Evaluation of Bibliographic Instruction: Lasting Encouragement." *College & Research Libraries* 42 (January 1981): 19–25.

Peterson, Lorna. *Measuring Students' Progress in Bibliographic Instruction: The Iowa State University Experience.* Ames, Ia.: Iowa State University, 1987. ERIC ED 293463.

Peterson, Lorna, and Jamie W. Coniglio. "Readability of Selected Academic Library Guides." *RQ* (Winter 1987): 233–39.

Phipps, Shelley, and Ruth Dickstein. "The Library Skills Program at the University of Arizona: Testing, Evaluation and Critique." *Journal of Academic Librarianship* 5 (September 1979): 205–14.

Powell, Ronald R. *Basic Research Methods for Librarians.* 2d ed. Norwood, N.J.: Ablex Publishing, 1991.

Puryear, Dorothy. "Computer-Aided Instruction for Literacy in Libraries." *Catholic Library World* 64 (October–March 1993–94): 40–42.

Rice, James, Jr. *Teaching Library Use: A Guide for Library Instruction.* Westport, Conn.: Greenwood Press, 1981.

Ridgeway, Trish, ed. *Improving Teaching and Training Techniques in Libraries.* New York: AMS Press, 1993.

Roberts, Anne F., and Susan G. Blandy. *Library Instruction for Librarians.* 2nd rev. ed. Englewood, Colo.: Libraries Unlimited, 1989.

Roberts, Anne F., and Susan G. Blandy. *Public Relations for Librarians.* Englewood, Colo.: Libraries Unlimited, 1989.

Shirato, Linda, ed. *Working with Faculty in the New Electronic Library.* Ann Arbor: Pierian Press, 1992.

Simmons-O'Neill, Elizabeth. "Evaluating Sources: Strategies for Faculty-Librarian-Student Collaboration." March 1990. ERIC ED 321259.

Simons, Michael. *Evaluation of Library Tours.* Reno: University of Nevada, Reno, <1990>. ERIC ED 331513.

Steenburgen-Gelb, Frances. *A Practical Guide to Writing Goals and Objectives.* Rev. ed. San Rafael, Calif.: Academic Therapy Publications, 1981.

Tiefel, Virginia. "Evaluating a Library User Education Program: A Decade of Experience." *College & Research Libraries* 50 (March 1989): 249–59.

Trail, Mary Ann, and Carolyn Gutierrez. "Evaluating a Bibliographic Instruction Program." *Research Strategies* 9 (Summer 1991): 124–29.

Turner, Philip M. "Evaluation." In *Helping Teachers Teach: A School Library Media Specialist's Role.* 2nd ed. Chicago: American Library Association, 1987.

Van House, Nancy A., et al. *Output Measures for Public Libraries: A Manual of Standardized Procedures.* 2nd ed. Chicago: American Library Association, 1987.

Walter, Virginia A. *Output Measures for Public Library Service to Children: A Manual of Standardization Procedures.* Chicago: American Library Association, 1992.

Welsch, Erwin K. "Technology and Library Instruction: The Potential of the Audio Visual Connection from IBM." *OCLC Micro* 6 (June 1990): 25–27.

Werking, Richard H. "Evaluating Bibliographic Education: A Review and Critique." *Library Trends* 29 (Summer 1980): 153–72.

Westbrook, Lynn, and Sharon DeDecker. "Supporting User Needs and Skills to Minimize Library Anxiety: Considerations for Academic Libraries." *Reference Librarian* 40 (1993): 43–51.

Index

Evaluation of This Handbook

Since this handbook was designed to improve the evaluation component of your library instruction, we would like you to tell us how you used it, how it was useful, and how it could have been more useful. As a librarian, your feedback is very valuable. Please take the time to answer the following questions and mail this to the name and address on the back of this form. Feel free to attach additional comments on another sheet.

1. My type of library is: *(Circle one.)*

    a) Academic
    b) Public
    c) School

    d) Special
    e) Other; please explain _____

2. I have been doing instruction for: *(Circle one.)*

    a) Less than two years
    b) Two to four years
    c) Five to seven years

    d) Eight to ten years
    e) More than ten years
    f) Does not apply

3. Evaluation is part of the planning process in my library. *(Circle one.)*

    Strongly agree   Strongly disagree

    1   2   3   4   5

4. This handbook was easy to use. *(Circle one.)*

    Strongly agree   Strongly disagree

    1   2   3   4   5

5. This handbook was well organized.

    Strongly agree   Strongly disagree

    1   2   3   4   5

6. Having the questions on a disk would have made this handbook more useful.

    Strongly agree   Strongly disagree

    1   2   3   4   5

7. I had trouble locating what I needed in this handbook.

    Strongly agree   Strongly disagree

    1   2   3   4   5

8. What did you find most useful about this handbook?

    What did you find least useful?

    What could have been added or deleted?

9. What other types of instructional tools would be helpful to you?

Thank you for your time and interest. Your feedback is invaluable!

FOLD HERE

CUT PAGE OUT

FOLD HERE

PLACE
STAMP
HERE

Sherry DeDecker
Davidson Library
University of California
Santa Barbara, CA 93106